Life Gave Me NO CHOICE

Life Gave Me NO CHOICE

Coretta Elaine Miller

Tampa, Florida

The content associated with this book is the sole work and responsibility of the author. Gatekeeper Press had no involvement in the generation of this content.

Life Gave Me NO CHOICE: The Making of A Super Woman

Published by Gatekeeper Press
7853 Gunn Hwy., Suite 209
Tampa, FL 33626
www.GatekeeperPress.com

Copyright © 2024 by Coretta Elaine Miller
All rights reserved. Neither this book, nor any parts within it may be sold or reproduced in any form or by any electronic or mechanical means, including information storage and retrieval systems, without permission in writing from the author. The only exception is by a reviewer, who may quote short excerpts in a review.

The cover design, interior formatting, typesetting, and editorial work for this book are entirely the product of the author. Gatekeeper Press did not participate in and is not responsible for any aspect of these elements.

Co-edited by Sweet, Sweet Spirit Publishing Company
Book Cover Photography Credit ~ Raw Exposure Photography
Bible Translations are New International Version (NIV) unless otherwise noted.

Library of Congress Control Number: 2024947123

ISBN (hardcover): 9781662957529
ISBN (paperback): 9781662957536
eISBN: 9781662957543

I dedicate this memoir to the woman I knew as Superwoman, my beloved mother, Alice T. Miller. May you continue to find rest in glory that life gave you no choice to find on earth. To my beloved daughters, the beats of my heart, my Guardian Angel and my Sunshine, I did this one for you. To all of my family, friends, and colleagues who said that I should write a book, cheers to you and the first of many others to come.

Table of Contents

Introduction/Foreword		1
Chapter 1:	My Superwoman	7
Chapter 2:	Carrying the Burden & Bearing the Weight	13
Chapter 3:	Blind in One Eye, Can't See out the Other	19
Chapter 4:	"Two All-Beef Patties, Special Sauce, Lettuce, Cheese . . ."	25
Chapter 5:	Deserted & Left Alone	29
Chapter 6:	Pursued by Grace	35
Chapter 7:	Understanding the Assignment	41
Chapter 8:	I Finally Cried!	47
Chapter 9:	My Lying Heart	53
Chapter 10:	The Makings for a Rainbow	61
Chapter 11:	A Taste of Glory	71
Chapter 12:	This Cape Doesn't Fit Anymore!	79
Chapter 13:	Taking the Cape Off & Retaining the Strength	91
Chapter 14:	Thank You, Dr. Pitters!	103
Chapter 15:	A Super Woman Pattern: Maintaining Purpose, Peace, and Balance	111

Introduction/Foreword

On the front of a T-shirt, I once read the phrase ***Behind every strong woman is a story that gave her No Choice***. The pages in this book tell the story of many life experiences that gave me no choice but to become the woman of strength that so many of my family members, friends, and colleagues see me as today. As I survived each experience, I gained the strength, perseverance, and tenacity to endure the next. You can say these life events and others became the fabric for the making of the Superwoman I would become known as, especially to my daughters. In many cases these were challenging and traumatic events that I experienced directly. The drastic nature of these experiences and my ability to persevere through them has led friends and associates over the years to encourage me to write a book about them.

In other instances, my Superwoman persona was cultivated through family traditions, cultural practices, and even the influence of religious doctrine. In my early childhood years, I was held to a higher standard of character within my inner and greater family circle. As the only girl among five children, I had to assume responsibilities within our family that my brothers didn't. This laid a foundation for me becoming the strong Black woman I am today. Not only was I tasked with these responsibilities over the years, but I was expected to succeed in fulfilling them. With the expectation to do well, I learned early how to excel at these and other tasks required of me. I was not given any awards or accolades, but over time I felt a sense of gratification and self-worthiness in just being able to accomplish these things.

That satisfaction also became my driving force for excelling in the things I did not have to do. I realized that I may not have had the things that made some girls in my neighborhood and those I went to school with popular, like a finely shaped body or name-brand fashions, but I could be smarter than most if I worked hard enough. In fifth grade, I remember hearing my school counselor tell my mom that I could get a scholarship to college if I kept making good grades, and that's exactly what I did.

My brothers were bigger and stronger than I was, and often used that advantage to push me around during our sibling fights. I learned how to overcome their advantage simply by outthinking them. Although I learned how to do most things like a boy, such as driving fast, preferring to wear pants instead of dresses, and working mechanical tools, when it came to overcoming challenges that my brothers presented, *I fought like a girl*! **When I couldn't beat them physically, I defeated them mentally!** For example, I once charged R.L., my second-oldest brother, an astronomical fee to iron his shirt when he was running late for a date one evening. "That's more than the dry cleaner charges!" he pouted. Knowing that the dry cleaner was closed, and I was his only option unless he be late for his date, I responded, "Well, take it to the cleaners then!" Having no other choice, he paid the fee.

My Uncle Sunny explained this relationship with my brothers best when he introduced me to a friend of the family recently while attending a family member's funeral. He began by saying, "Talking bout somebody smart!" He explained further that when I was a little girl and he came down to our house, I would say, "Uncle Sunny, I ain't got time to be fooling around with them boys; I gots to get my lesson! And got her lesson she did . . . She was something else, I tell you, and still is," he proudly exclaimed! Joyfully laughing, he added, "She knew how to keep dem brothers of hers in order too!"

This was the standard set when I was a child, and it remains today. I was reminded again in a text message from my mom's youngest brother a few months ago that read, "Good Morning, this is your uncle Bubba just sitting here drinking my coffee thinking about what a phenomenal woman you are . . .!" Over the years, life would dictate my transformation from Uncle Sunny's "little smart girl" to Uncle Bubba's "phenomenal woman." It didn't happen as easily as some would think, such as my youngest daughter, who wrote in her 2024 Instagram Mother's Day tribute to me, "I don't know how you do it, because it's always done."

As many of the stories to follow will reflect, I have had to walk out the famous words "only the *strong* survive!" Whether in obedience to parental authority, adherence to cultural and religious tradition, or in response to life's misfortunes and tragedies, life gave me *no choice* but to be Superwoman in the practical sense and to protect my emotional well-being. This became my default mode of existing and led to feelings of gratification and worthiness. So even when I didn't have to be Superwoman, I did because it felt natural and good!

This revelation came while I was in seminary. In my Pastoral Care course, we studied the work of Chanequa Walker-Barnes titled *Too Heavy a Yoke*. From the beginning, I saw myself in the book as I shared with my professor and fellow seminarians! My life to that point was summed up in what Barnes terms the "StrongBlackWoman," one word, not three. She defines the "StrongBlackWoman" as a "legendary figure, typified by extraordinary capabilities for caring and suffering without complaint," built on a "cultural myth that has defined and confined ways of being in the world for women of African descent." Yet Barnes notes that there is a difference in being a "StrongBlackWoman" and a Black woman who happens to be strong, having the ability to demonstrate an abundance of physical, emotional, and/or spiritual strength that preserves them through seasons of adversity and tragedy. The "StrongBlackWoman" she contrasts as a fixed character" or "scripted role" based on cultural traditions and religious ideologies of which Black women are reared and molded into, usually from childhood. She was talking about me.

This life-breathing revelation inspired me to embark upon a journey to transform my life and my living from being a

Superwoman to that of a super woman, two words, not one; a woman who utilizes her gifts, talents, and strengths with wisdom and purpose to not only survive life's crises but to thrive as a result thereof. A journey to take off the cape or fixed ideology of the Superwoman character I had embodied, yet retain the strength that had been demonstrated through it that I may purposefully and wisely use in times of need.

This was crucial not only to restoring and maintaining my well-being but also that of my daughters, who for most of their lives beheld me as their *Superwoman*. My oldest daughter, having witnessed me endure some of life's toughest challenges, had become convinced that there was nothing humanly possible I could not do if I chose to do it! Meanwhile, it became apparent that my youngest daughter had inherited many of my personality traits that would easily aid her into becoming a Superwoman, especially having her mother as a live pattern to follow as I had in my mother. In hopes of changing that trajectory, I sought to refine the pattern for being a strong or super woman.

This journey would require critical reflection and self-examination to realize that while many of my life experiences gave me no choice but to embody strength and perseverance to survive them, in some of the cases where I did have a choice, I could have chosen wiser. The making of a super woman would also call for some spiritual and theological reflection to reexamine traditional religious beliefs and Biblical teachings that cultivated a pattern for becoming a Superwoman, such as Proverbs 31. I committed to transforming my views concerning the role of a strong Godly woman by finding renewal and hope in scriptural texts to liberate women, especially those who were ostracized and marginalized, such as Queen Vashti in the book of Esther and Hagar in the book of Genesis.

The lessons learned and insights gained from this journey, I share in the pages of this book, with prayers that my daughters and others who find that life's circumstances give them *no choice* but to be a *Superwoman* will find hope and liberation to be super women instead.

Chapter 1
My Superwoman

My first *superhero* was not a cartoon or comic book character. She didn't wear a fancy costume with a cape nor crown on her head, but to me she had *superpowers*. She overcame obstacles and challenges she never should have and defied the odds set against her. She demonstrated strength beyond what a woman like herself normally would and never seemed to stop working. Every time life knocked her down, my *Superwoman* bounced right back up! She prospered beyond what her salary as a maid could afford and excelled above what her high school education in rural Alabama taught her. My *Superwoman* was my mom. In her life, my pattern for being a Superwoman was laid in the same way I remember her laying the Simplicity and Butterick fabric patterns out on her bed for the clothes she made for me. Behind her strength was a life that gave her *no choice*!

She was the "virtuous woman" of Proverbs 31 and had the survival instincts of Ruth in the Bible. She watched over the affairs of our household—cooking, cleaning, ironing, sewing, painting, repairing—and even before she and my dad divorced, she also went out each day to do the same in the homes of the people for which she worked. Whether in the cotton fields of

Washington County, Alabama, the private homes she worked in, or as a custodian at The Alabama Department of Transportation, she prided herself and her worth in her work. Nobody cleaned better than she did, and her ironing could put any dry cleaner out of business!

Life in our family was good until I turned about eight or nine years old. We weren't, as we used to say, "dirt poor," but we lived on the lower end of the socioeconomic scale. We lived in our own two-bedroom house that my parents were buying, and we didn't have to rely on government funding while they were married. My parents were the typical hardworking American-dream-seeking couple until my Daddy strayed outside of their marriage. As the affair began to negatively impact his life, he took it out on my mom. I watched Mom endure emotional and physical abuse at the hands of my father. I remember he became angry with her when he failed to show up to work because he was out all night with his mistress, and when his supervisor called, my mom told him that my father wasn't home. On another occasion, he was actually home but didn't go to work, and because he had cursed and scolded her before for telling his supervisor he wasn't home, she gave him the phone this time. She was cursed and scolded the same way. The plate of food she had cooked and served him in bed, he threw back at her! She was damned if she did and damned if she didn't. I witnessed him hitting her and even held my breath on one occasion as I watched him intimidate her by pulling his gun out during an argument. But every time life knocked my mom down, the *Superwoman* in her bounced right back up.

When life gave her no choice, she did what it took to not only survive but, in many instances, thrive as a result. With the legal separation she preferred no longer an option, she divorced my dad when I was ten years old. When he left, our home mortgage was three payments behind! But my *Superwoman* went into action, borrowed the money from her employers, and worked the balance off until there was none. Even though Dad rarely paid child support, she later renovated that same home to adequately accommodate the size our family and increased its value. My dad left us without a car. Momma didn't even know how to drive then, but she walked and rode the bus to work and wherever she needed to go until she could purchase a car. By the time my father passed away about eleven or twelve years later, she had experienced car ownership numerous times!

Then her diligence and hard work earned her a piece of the American dream with the purchase of her forever home. It became her canvas to paint a masterfully decorated, immaculate masterpiece in a home that at the time of her death was valued at nearly five times what she purchased it for, and you could eat off its floors and yard! She retired about ten years after its purchase. She had nothing to fear concerning financial stability. But Momma kept on working, taking on part-time jobs, and paid her mortgage off years before it was due. In all of this, she continued to worship and faithfully serve the Lord!

This exemplary display of strength, perseverance, and faith was inherently passed down from my mother to me, I explained to my counselor. Idleness, complacency, and failure just weren't in my DNA! As the only girl, there were just certain duties that were expected of me. Yet there were certain character traits in her that I idolized. As I matured into a woman and especially a mother, I appreciated the *Superwoman* I had in my mother and held her example as a standard to live by. "*You are my hero*, I strive for the life of hard work, spiritual devotion to God, and morality that you live," I wrote in a tribute for her retirement celebration in 2004. When she asked me if I needed her to come be with me when I got divorced, I said, "No, Momma. I got this." I was a whole grown woman with a successful career as a nurse practitioner. If she thrived off so much less, surely, I could do the same, I thought, as the stories to follow will reflect.

However, in 2020, my *Superwoman* lost her physical strength as her heart failed her. She stopped breathing and had to be resuscitated twice. Even while on a ventilator, her heart stopped functioning three times and had to be revived. It was not a heart attack from clogged arteries, but rather heart failure caused by physical exertion, the doctor explained. My *Superwoman* had worked her heart to the point of death! **The *strength* built to keep her and protect her all these years was now the *strength* that had broken her.** If only she had learned to *rest*.

Each day for about two weeks as I got off the elevator on my way to the ICU unit where she was hospitalized, I asked God to prepare me for what I was about to face as I witnessed the critical nature of my mom's condition firsthand. One day I arrived just as they had revived her heart, others I spent watching her heart go in and out of deadly rhythms. Through it all, I thought if God allowed me to reach the nearly seventy-nine years she had, I would hope it would not end because I had worked myself to death . . . that I could learn to *rest.*

By the grace and mercy of God, the placement of a pacemaker and defibrillator in her heart was successful and she survived. Yet she still couldn't seem to find rest unless she was working! This I saw firsthand during the six weeks she spent with me after she was discharged from rehab. Once she got her strength back, she was up and working in any way or wherever she could find! When I insisted that she not do certain things, she would just mope around, saying once, "Well what I am supposed to do then?" I came to understand then that moving forward, I needed to make a few alterations in the *Superwoman* pattern she had laid for me.

INSIGHT

Superheroes **need rest too! Even God rested after the creation. "For whoever enters God's rest also rests from his own work, just as God did from His."**
—Hebrews 4:10

Practical Tools for Finding Rest

- *Schedule* a time to find *spiritual rest*, in addition to physical rest each day . . . listen to relaxing music, for meditation, read the Bible, and/or *always pray*.
- *Set boundaries* and stick to them, leave some work for another day or someone else to do, and learn how to say *no* and mean it.
- *Strive* for excellence, and accept that doing your best is good enough, understanding that even when we fall short, God will perfect those things concerning us to fulfill His purpose for our lives. (Psalm 138:8)

Chapter 2
Carrying the Burden & Bearing the Weight

"It's a shame I have to go to work and clean and come home and cleanup too," my mom cried! I tried to explain that I had vacuumed the floors in our house several times during that day, but each time, some of my brothers kept messing it back up. But she did not believe me and continued to complain as she began to vacuum the floor. Feeling convicted, as if I had done wrong, I reached for the vacuum to finish the job, and as I grabbed the hose it accidentally hit her. Of course, she thought I purposely hit her, and cried even more!

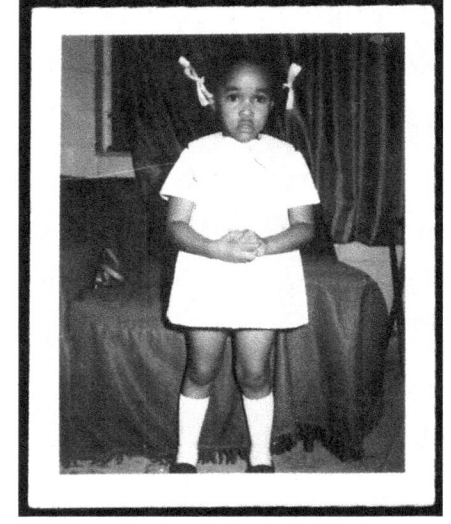

There was absolutely no way I would have even thought about hitting *my* momma, who did not believe in sparing the rod by any means. I flipped off at the mouth at times, like any other teen, but I honored my mother. Nevertheless, since she thought I hit her, I was certain to get a beating as if I had stolen something! I ran to my room, packed a few clothes, and pushed the dresser to the window so that if I had to, I could climb out, but she never came in the room.

This was a typical day in the life of our family, especially after my parents divorced. As the only girl, I was not spoiled as many people may think, not even in the least! Instead, I was held to a higher standard of doing just about everything than that of my brothers. It's not that I was favored or given much more than any of them so that much more would be expected of me, because I was not. It just was!

Early on I had to assume responsibility for many of the household chores usually shared only with my mom. Sometimes my oldest brother D.W. would feel sorry for me and help with washing dishes, but as he got older, he was often away from the house either working or taking part in school sports activities and eventually moved to another state when I was a young teen. My other three brothers, who were both older and younger than me, did not have to wash dishes nor do any other housework on a regular basis.

This was influenced by cultural beliefs held by my mom and my dad that certain household duties were seen as "women's work." It didn't matter that my brothers outnumbered me by four times. It was the standard my mom held herself to as a woman and expected the same of me. My father didn't help the matter either, especially after the divorce. He would tell my mom not to be making his boys (which excluded my oldest brother) do that "women's work." Even when my mom's family members and friends would tell her that it wasn't fair to me that my brothers helped make the mess but didn't have to share in cleaning it up, she never made them do it. They were not made to do it, and they didn't.

Sometimes just to taunt me they would purposely dirty up the place even if I had already cleaned it for the day. For example, if I locked the front door to keep them from tracking dirt on the floors that I had cleaned, then they would come through the back door and go back out of the front tracking dirt just the same. This meant while my brothers and other children were outdoors playing, I was usually inside cleaning. I couldn't participate in sports, band, or other extracurricular activities because I always had to go home after school to do my chores. I learned then how to work harder, faster, and smarter so I could have some time to play.

As I got older, the responsibilities increased, including caring for my baby brother, especially after my mom took on an evening job during my high school years. Whatever I did for myself, I had to do for him: from making sure he ate dinner and took a bath to ironing and preparing his clothes for school. Even though I was seven years older than him, I was still a child. I got an early taste of what being a superwoman was like.

Even when I hadn't done well, my parents assumed that I had. In school I was expected to get good grades probably because I almost always excelled beyond my brothers. Yet I wasn't rewarded for doing so. They just expected that I would. Along with and because of their expectations, I carried the weight and pressure of meeting a standard that I didn't even understand nor knew how the weight and pressure would shape the rest of my life.

I remember feeling that my brothers who got in trouble received more attention for misbehaving than I did for doing well. My mom took off work to come to the school when they got in trouble, but rarely came for any of my class programs. My father always found the money to cover his sons' juvenile delinquencies, but never had any to support my doing well. I purposely didn't perform my best in my least favorite subject—English Literature—during my sophomore year of high school. I received a *D* in the class that quarter. But as I road home, I feared what might happen and changed it to a *B*. When I got home, my mother never even asked to see my report card, because she assumed that I had done well. The next morning, I changed the *B* back to a *D*, signed her name, and returned it to school. I had to retake that class the next year because I was in an advanced studies track and had to earn a *C* or better in my course classes to get credit.

Lesson learned: I should not let others be the motivation for me excelling or failing. In all that I was made to do and expected to do during my childhood, the truth is I was very bright and intellectually gifted anyway! I had already begun to manifest the God-given strength and character to succeed in life regardless of whether my mother or anyone else celebrated me for doing so or not.

From that point forward, I've tried my best academically even when I haven't made the grade I wanted. So often we do not walk in our God-ordained gifts and talents, because we become distracted or overwhelmed by the circumstances of life. By the grace of God in this case and others, not only did I escape punishment from my mother had she known what I had done, but my poor judgment did not keep me from excelling enough to complete my dream of going to college and earning a scholarship to do so.

> **INSIGHT**
> Never shrink or play yourself small to appease or get the attention of others, nor allow the circumstances of life to deter you from manifesting your God-given talents and gifts. Instead, let your dreams and hopes be your focus and keep you motivated for doing well, especially when facing adversity. As Galatians 6:9 encourages, "Let us not become weary in doing good, for the proper time we will reap a harvest if we do not give up."

Chapter 3
Blind in One Eye, Can't See out the Other

There were incidents experienced in my childhood that could or should have destroyed me, yet like with my mother, overcoming these obstacles actually gave me the strength to overcome future challenges. Though I failed to understand as I do now that it was the Grace of God that protected me, surviving these traumatic events actually fueled or fed the *Superwoman* spirit within.

"M.J., stop poking me in my eye with that pencil," I screamed over and over in my sleep! M.J., knowing that he wasn't poking me with anything, looked down from the top bunk to the bottom where I was sleeping, only to be startled by what he saw. My left eye was swollen as large as a golf ball with blood streaming from it. It was no poking of a pencil in my eye that I felt, but rather the throbbing pain of the BB rippling through my left eye socket. My three-year-old baby brother M.T. had shot me with an older brother's BB gun while playing "cowboys and Indians." The gun wasn't even supposed to be in the house, much less have any BBs in it!

Fearful of the whooping they were surely to get once Mom returned home from choir rehearsal, R.L. convinced M.J. that the BB didn't go in my eye, but rather had just grazed my face. And instead of calling or taking me to my grandmother who lived just a few houses up the street, I was made to lay in pain for what felt like an eternity, until my mom came back home. The BB was in my eye, and I had to spend my entire week of spring break in the University of South Alabama hospital. I remember my oldest brother D.W. came by with treats. He was still in high school, but old enough to drive and have a part-time job.

The doctors decided to leave the BB where it was because I had some sight remaining in that eye, but enough damage had been done to declare me legally blind in that eye, a status that remains today. I can see things in general but there's no acuity of sight. I can read the big *E* on top of the eye chart, but that's about it. I remember hearing the doctors tell my mom that I would have to be careful with my good eye from then on, because if I ever injured it, I would be completely blind. That advice I haven't exactly followed, especially wearing the glasses he prescribed to strengthen my "good eye."

The injury caused that eye to become lazy, and all of the "cocked eye" jokes I received afterward, some by the same brothers who were culprits in the matter, was all the ridicule my young prideful heart could withstand. Being teased about the huge ugly glasses my Mama bought for me and insisted I wear, I also could have done without. So, I didn't wear them when I was out of my mom's eyesight, except on school picture day. That way, she'd think I'd been wearing them at school all along. Over the years, I learned to compensate for the loss, like reading out of the same eye for my driver's license test, for fear I wouldn't pass if they knew I couldn't see well out of that eye. For pictures, I would always turn to that side and hope the lazy eye wouldn't stray before the picture was taken, and I styled my hair over that eye during those days to hide it. Eventually I had corrective surgery in my young adulthood to straighten the injured eye.

Yet, as the doctor predicted, the wear and tear on my "good eye" took its toll, and I would eventually need corrective glasses to be able to see well in that eye also. By the *grace* of God, I have not experienced any injury or physical harm to my "good eye" over the years; nonetheless, the spirit of the trauma remained. Though it was an accident, no one considered the fear, hurt, anger, doubt, and brokenness I must have felt even at that age. I trusted my older brothers who were there to protect me, and they let this happen. Now, how would I trust them? How would I trust others? However, life resumed as normal for my family; my parents went back to work, and I went back to school, but it was and will never be normal for me. I had *no choice* but to make sense of what happened to me on my own.

But with every physical and emotional act of trauma, there is a spirit of trauma that it embodies; for example, rape personifies a spirit of control and power. Though it was just a BB that pierced my eye, my mind and spirit were wounded even more so. Every time I was teased about being "cross-eyed," I relived the trauma. I don't recall my brothers receiving any severe punishment like I felt they should either, only that they couldn't have any more guns until they were adults. But my dad blamed my momma because she was not at home when it happened. Instead of addressing the problem, which was my brother's disobedience in bringing the gun in the house, I wasn't allowed to stay home alone with the boys anymore until I was in my older teenage years, as if it was my fault that I was shot. Wherever my mom went outside of work, I was with her, unless I stayed with my grandma or another adult. I felt like I had been shot again.

> **INSIGHT**
>
> Too often children are left to process trauma and loss, such as the death of loved ones, without any therapeutic counseling or even acknowledgment of what they're feeling. And in many instances, the spirit of that trauma and loss resurfaces in the lives of these children as relationship dysfunction, poor academic performance, and/or as I have witnessed with many of my pediatric patients, they resort to acts of violence and delinquent behaviors. I can't stress enough the importance of being able to grieve in times of loss. "Blessed are those who mourn," the Bible teaches us, "because they will be comforted" (Matthew 5:4). Although He went on to raise Lazarus from the dead, even Jesus took the time to grieve the loss of his friend, and those who witnessed it, acknowledged his loss and expressed sympathy for him, the Gospel of John writes (11:33–35).

Chapter 4
"Two All-Beef Patties, Special Sauce, Lettuce, Cheese..."

A few years later, I experienced a robbery at a McDonald's restaurant. "Two all-beef patties, special sauce, lettuce, cheese, on a sesame seed bun," rang so loudly in my head as I patiently waited for my Big Mac, that I didn't even process what the man next to me was saying. I heard the robber say to the worker while he pointed what looked to be a gun under his jacket at me, "You better give me all the money if you don't want this little girl to get hurt!" But I didn't process what was really happening until the robbers ran out of the restaurant with the money and D.W., my oldest brother, who had been waiting in the car, rushed in.

"Why did you just stand there waiting on that stupid hamburger?" he frantically screamed at me as he checked to make sure I was ok. I was fine or at least appeared to be. I waited because rarely did I get an opportunity to eat out, and I don't remember whether someone had given me the money or I had earned it in some way, but I was determined not to have to eat Mom's cooking that evening. I hated Mom's homemade burgers; they were fat with big onion pieces sticking out, and the juice always made the white sandwich bread wet! So, having an opportunity to get a real burger was a rare treat. I imagined it would taste just like it looked on the TV!

D.W. was old enough to drive and had given me a ride to the fast-food restaurant that evening. He helplessly watched the whole thing unfold from the car and was quite traumatized by it. "Had I come in, the robbers would have shot her and me!" he desperately tried to explain to my mother when we got home. Maybe he felt a sense of guilt, that he couldn't protect me in that moment. He was seven years older than I was and had taken on a caretaker role for me and our youngest brother after my parents divorced. Maybe it was just the fear of what could have happened that had him so upset! However, I appeared unfazed by it! And yes, I ate my Big Mac too! I had waited a long time for this, of course I was going to eat it, but I don't recall it tasting as good as I thought it would.

The spirit of the trauma I experienced and witnessed to this point of my life loomed heavily here. I was not supposed to be fazed by the emotional and physical violence my mother endured at the hands of my father toward the end of their marriage, including threatening her with a gun. I was not supposed to be fazed by the BB gunshot injury to my eye, and all of its aftereffects. So why would I be fazed by this? Well, I was! I just appeared undisturbed at the time.

INSIGHT

Although each of these events were separate and different in their own way, the emotional trauma associated with each were one and the same. When we fail to acknowledge and address the pain, fear, anger, grief, depression, anxiety, and other emotional brokenness associated with traumatic events such as those that I endured, this spirit of the trauma remains, even when the physical act no longer exists. Unfortunately, the dysfunctional means of coping lingers also. The stress of this and all the traumatic experiences I endured and my response to them or the lack thereof would eventually take its toll. Even though I didn't cry or outwardly grieve in response to these traumatic events, like my mother did with cleaning, I developed behaviors that mimicked OCD (obsessive compulsive disorder) as ways of coping with anxiety and stress. Organizing things in the midst of chaos brought me peace of mind and spirit. I've learned while in grief counseling that this was not the reflection of an anxiety disorder as I had diagnosed myself with, but more that of PTSD (post-traumatic stress disorder).

Chapter 5
Deserted & Left Alone

After I was shot in the eye, my mother rarely let me stay home with the boys nor did she allow me to go out without her or another adult she trusted going with me. But on this particular Friday evening, she finally let me go out with my friends. We met at the Murphy High vs Vigor High football game. My brothers R.L. and M.J. were given permission to drive the family car provided they looked out for me. I didn't expect them to hang out with me and my friends, nor did I want them to. I just never thought they would leave the football stadium without me!

I waited and waited pacing back and forth. I even walked around the entire perimeter of the stadium, but my brothers were nowhere to be found nor was my mom's car. I used to be ashamed of it because it was old, big, and ugly, but oh I wished I would have seen that green Plymouth. Meanwhile, my friends all left, and Ladd stadium looked like someone had pressed the fast-forward button, as it seemingly went from full to empty in a manner of seconds. Even the workers left after a while. Oh, how I wished I'd paid attention when my cousins and I walked past Ladd Stadium many times before on our way to the convenience store from their house. Even though my mom's sister lived just a few blocks away, I could not remember how to get there. And if I left, I would miss my brothers who I just knew would be back to get me at any moment, so I stayed.

At first, he walked past me, but he doubled back and asked what I was doing out there all alone. I lied and said that my brothers were just on the other side of the stadium and would be around to pick me up any moment. He left and I don't remember how long, but sometime later he came back by and when he realized I was still all alone, he tried to seduce me into having sex with him. He wasn't an old man, but he was much older and stronger than I was! I wasn't old enough to drive yet, so I had to be around fourteen years old or so. Of course, I was a virgin and probably still had my Barbie doll collection then, but I didn't want to say no to him for fear he would harm me. I remembered reading or hearing on TV somewhere that rape was really a power trip, so I began to make excuses as to why we couldn't just have sex there, like "not out in the open on the concrete in the parking lot!" All the while, I was crying and praying within that God would send somebody, anybody to rescue me. I was more afraid than I was when the robber at McDonald's threatened to harm me.

The more excuses I made, the more irritated he became with me and he began to physically force me toward a grassy area he found. But each time he pulled and pushed me, by the grace of God, a car passed by, and he would take his hands off me and act as if we were together. Yet none of the cars were my mom's car, and the people in them were not my brothers nor anyone I knew or even the police. Then finally, after what seemed to be an eternity, I recognized the driver of the car that pulled up. It was the older male cousin of my childhood BFF, Annick. I was never so happy to see someone.

As I walked in the door of our house, my mother scolded me because my brothers told her I was not at the stadium when they looked for me and must have gotten a ride with my friends. I swore to her that I didn't leave the stadium, but I didn't share what happened while I waited. Maybe if I had and she had listened, she would have realized I was telling the truth. But I did not tell her. I just sucked it up, like when she would fuss at me for not cleaning up the house when the truth was that I had, but these same brothers would mess it back up.

It really didn't matter whether she believed me or not because no whipping nor punishment I could have received from her would have been worse than what I imagined would have happened to me if the grace and mercy of God did not protect me that night. I've never shared this story with anyone until now. Nor have I cried the tears I now shed as I write it. I share and cry now for the little girl in me who learned how not to cry but just suck it up and move on when I faced hurtful experiences like this. Even then the lining of my *Superwoman* persona was being made.

Recounting this experience makes me sorrowfully mindful of the countless souls who were not as fortunate as me, who have experienced rape and other sexual violence and never told anyone. I am also made conscious of those who have been brave and courageous enough to tell their story but were not believed, who have never had anyone advocate for them and validate their truth, nor even acknowledge their trauma. Instead, many have been called liars and punished for what they had no control over happening to them. To *all* these souls, I hear your *truth*, acknowledge your *trauma*, and offer this prayer for your *pain*.

Prayer Of Comfort

God who is our Deliverer! Who has been and forever will be the Redeemer of our souls. We boldly approach your throne of grace and mercy that we may lay petitions at your feet on behalf of all your children who have been violated and victimized through rape, molestation, and other sexual violence, that you will grant them a portion of your grace that is sufficient to cover whatever physical or emotional affliction their trauma may have caused. Wherever they are weakened, let your strength be perfected in them. Restore them where they feel empty, void, and violated, as only you can; make them whole again where they have been broken in body, mind, spirit, and heart, oh great Potter you are, that they will be used by you to be a testimony of their deliverance to other victims. Grant them peace that stills and silences the storms within. And when the enemy comes in with its flood of malicious lies, false accusations, and wrongful condemnation, we pray that your Spirit, Oh Lord, will raise up of a standard of truth, vindication, and redemption, for you are the God of all truth and know all things. In the name of the one You sent to heal the brokenhearted, preach deliverance to the captives, recover sight to the blind, and set at liberty them that are bruised, Jesus the Christ, we pray!

Chapter 6
Pursued by Grace

"Oh my God, we thought your car was surely going over the edge of the freeway," the people cried as they rushed toward me, some checking to see if I had any injuries; others were amazed that I was still alive.

I was spending the summer after my first year of college with D.W. and his wife in Dallas, Texas, so that I could work and save money to buy better automobile insurance for my new Chevrolet Sprint. I'd gotten insurance with the purchase of the car, but the monthly payment was more than originally quoted, and I couldn't afford both it and my car payment on my income as a part-time nursing assistant. In my youthful indiscretion, I dropped it and carried only the mandatory minimum coverage required by GMAC, which was the financing company, until I could get better. My mom agreed to add me on her Allstate policy since I was still living in her household. It would be cheaper and better coverage, but I had to make the payments and provide the initial down payment. My brother and sister-in-law encouraged me to come to Dallas and work at the hospital where my sister-in-law worked as a registered nurse. I would earn much more working in the same position. I did and chose to work in the Surgical Intensive Care Unit (SICU).

Things were going well. I was saving my money and almost had enough to send back to my mom. I had just gained enough confidence to drive on the freeways and decided to drive to the neighboring town of Seagoville to visit my new friend, the niece of my sister-in-law. In an abundance of caution, I was driving in the center lane of the multi-lane freeway, when suddenly I noticed that a car in the second lane to my left was making a beeline for the exit that was two lanes to my right. I sped up to get out of his way, but not quick enough to prevent his car from tapping my rear bumper. It was only a tap, but it was enough force to send my car fishtailing across the busy freeway. The portion of the interstate I was driving on was overlapping and was so high in the air that I could only see clouds and the tops of skyscrapers out of my front windshield as my car spun uncontrollably toward the outer railing of the freeway. There were several cars driving on the freeway, but miraculously none came within three or four car radiuses of me during the time that my car was spinning across the lanes. It was as if suddenly their vehicles were paused.

I remembered that my father and brothers had cautioned me against slamming on the brakes when the vehicle is spinning uncontrollably as mine was. So, I tried to gain control with the steering wheel, and when that failed, I pulled the emergency brake, but to no avail. When it became evident that my car would inevitably crash into and through the freeway's railing, I took my hands off the steering wheel, crossed them over my heart, closed my eyes and said, "Here I come, Lord!" Oddly, I don't recall feeling afraid to die. I was only nineteen years old at the time, and way too young to die, right? But I was sure, as well as all who witnessed the accident, that my car would not only crash into the barrier, but would likely continue through it, over the edge of the freeway and ultimately crashing countless feet to the ground and to my death. It seemed. But God!

My car did crash into the barrier! It was so light that a mere tap on my rear bumper sent it fishtailing across the highway. That weakness would become my saving *grace*. Because it was so light, it lacked the weight to go through the railing, but instead repelled and spun backward. When I opened my eyes, I was back in the middle of the freeway! None of the cars were anywhere near me, including the one that hit mine. Witnesses said the man driving the other car kept going. But God had encamped his angels around me, who stayed with me until the police and my brother got there.

I didn't fully appreciate the *grace* and mercy of God covering me then; I was more concerned about my car. Of course, it was totaled! As we drove away from the accident, my brother and sister-in-law worried about my physical well-being, but I worried about how I would get another car to drive back and forth to class and to my clinical nursing assignments. They didn't know that the insurance coverage I had would not replace my car, but I did. It would get worse before it got better from there. The insurance that GMAC required me to get did not pay the balance owed on my car loan as they said it would. The car was not drivable the way it was, and there was no way I could afford to repair it. My account was forced into a voluntary repossession for the balance. Now I had no car and damaged credit! GMAC claimed the insurance they required that was supposed to cover the remaining balance was not enough, so I was responsible for that difference as well.

I would have to live with the limitations the repossession placed on my credit for several years, yet the grace of God pursued me even then. My mom assisted me in getting another car as soon as I got back home. I finished working through the summer in Dallas, and when I returned home, we went to her bank. Because of her excellent credit history with them, and my good credit report prior to the accident, the bank financed a used car for me, a red Mazda GLC. It was like new because the previous owner hardly drove it because he was usually away on military duty.

The voluntary repossession was always a blemish on my credit report whenever I applied for any type of credit, including apartment applications, but God always had a ram in the bush. About four years afterward, someone filed a class action lawsuit against GMAC that ultimately cleared my credit. By now I'd become accustomed to adversity, dealing with my credit—with life in general—as well as the grace and mercy of God that usually accompanied it.

From the car accident, I began learning how to walk in that *grace*. I remained steadfast in my studies and continued the path to become a registered nurse. And even during the time that my credit score was damaged by the repossession, I still protected it, paying whatever bills I had on time as if it had not been damaged. To do otherwise, I would have forsaken the grace of God that protected my life in the accident. This was crucial because once my credit was cleared by the lawsuit, my excellent credit score was restored, which was just in time for us to be able to finance our first home.

Too often people become disheartened by their misfortunes in life and give up on their dreams and on God. Some even turn away from God and his ways to a life of worldliness instead. Yet these are the times when we must cling to the promises of God and trust in His Word. It is easy to trust God when things are going well, but the true test of our faith is trusting Him when we can't see or trace Him working in our lives.

Like with Job in the Bible, sometimes God allows us to go through trials and tribulations just to see if we will trust Him to get us through it. In all the adversity and devastation Job went through, he never cursed God as his wife suggested, nor did he turn away from doing right in the eyes of the Lord. As a result of his faith, God blessed him with twice as much as he had before. I also watched my mom triumph over many of life's obstacles by faith, lending and depending on the Lord. So, when misfortune found me, I had *no choice* but to follow her pattern.

INSIGHT

Sometimes the strength others see in us as *superpower* is simply the *grace* of God. Regardless of how gifted, righteous, or upright we are or how much hard work we do, if not for the grace of God, some experiences in life would simply destroy us. This experience taught me how to appreciate that grace.

A Prayer for Perseverance

Our Lord who is our Shepherd, and we are your sheep. We call upon you in these troubling times, because your Word assures us that if we call upon you, you will answer and be with us in trouble and will deliver and honor us. Help us to hold on to this promise when it's hard to see the works of your hand, trusting and believing that even when we are afflicted and troubled, you will deliver us of them all. Allow us to hear your voice and feel your presence when we can't see You. Hold us in the palm of your hands that no one or nothing we go through will take us from you. Oh Lord, Our Strength and Our Redeemer. Amen.

Chapter 7
Understanding the Assignment

"*B*reathe, man, breathe," my fitness trainer yelled at me during a workout session, with no disrespect to my gender intended! "I *am*," I replied. "You're not breathing, because you don't want to feel the pain, but you have to *breathe* through the pain," he scolded! He was right. Of course I was breathing or else I wouldn't be alive, but not fully. I came to realize that this was my way of dealing with painful and stressful situations. Thus, whenever I anticipated tense or painful situations, I unknowingly would just hold my breath. In the midst of a traffic jam, rushing to get out the door for work or church, in anticipation of bad news, or the painful sting of lifting heavy weights, I would inhale, but failed to get the maximum benefits of breathing by exhaling. It's like with swimming, taking a breath of air before going underwater and holding your breath until you resurface above water again, or in my case until the pain or intense situation subsides.

Likewise, I'd gained a reputation since my childhood for being one that didn't cry much. Failing to release the hurt through tears, I internalized it. Two ineffective means of coping with pain and stress. I don't know how long I'd been compromising my air and well-being with either behavior to avoid feeling the emotional and physical pains of life. Maybe as early as when my father would hit my mother, and perceiving her tears as weakness, thought she should fight back instead of crying. This would explain my nonchalant response to the traumatic events of my preteen and teen years. I don't know, but this internalizing of pain and fear I had surely mastered in my childhood, because when I was twenty-three years old, my father passed away, and I didn't shed a tear.

I'd been convincing myself all these years that I felt no loss within his death because I'd lost him years before. Not in the physical sense but in all that matters when it comes to having a father. From the time he and my mother divorced, he failed to be the provider, protector, and supporter I'd known and trusted him to be. From that time in high school when I asked him for money to pay fees so that I could take the examination to be exempted from English 101 in my freshmen year of college, and he said he didn't have it nor made any effort to get it—I felt fatherless. I responded by saying, "Maybe you can get it from the same place you get money to get your sons out of trouble." As I tearfully pouted my way down my grandmother's long driveway, I added, "If you can't help me when I need you, then I don't need a daddy." It was this loss of my father I thought I had already grieved as a child, thus no need to cry at his death.

However, in retrospect the loss to mourn his death was not about the father he had and had not been to me as a child, but rather about the father he would never ever be able to be again, and that's the loss I just couldn't bear. So, whereas it hurt me to see my grandmother cry at the gravesite as they committed his body back to the earth, I *did not cry*, and thereby nullified the loss. At least I thought.

I would, however, cry when I lost my first baby on October 21, 1993. In my eleventh week of pregnancy, I had been having some light bleeding after playing tennis one day. Yet over and over my doctor assured me that I was fine and encouraged me to continue working and going about my daily activities as I had been doing. But something was very wrong! I was actually leaking amniotic fluid, the water surrounding the baby that nourishes and protects it. By the time my doctor realized it, it was too late.

At the twentieth week, my fluid eventually dropped below levels viable for survival, and she died. After working a twelve-hour shift at the hospital, I awakened in extreme pain. By the time we got to the emergency room, she was almost out, I couldn't walk, nor could I sit in the wheelchair they used to transport me to the labor and delivery unit. It was too late to put me to sleep or even do an epidural. The doctor encouraged me to push as he pulled my baby girl out.

I cried outwardly and inwardly because I felt the emotional and physical pain of the loss. It hurt and this time I cried. My husband who was waiting outside the door could hear me cry out. He explained that the nurses, assuming we were not married but just another unmarried Black teenage couple, made him wait outside. Even if we had been, that excuse had no merit; he had been there when she was conceived! Nonetheless, he didn't insist on coming in to be by my side. The doctor gave me Valium in hopes that it would ease some of the trauma of the experience, but it didn't. I remember it all.

She was beautiful. She was fully formed, having all ten of her toes and fingers, but her eyes were still closed. She was only a few grams from the weight that the law requires for resuscitation. I named her Maya Alaina. I didn't get a chance to hold her, but I have pictures. They asked me if I wanted to see her as soon as they pulled her out, but in that moment, I was alone and afraid, so I said no.

Later when her father said that he held her, I told him I wanted to see her before they disposed of her body, but he discouraged me, saying he didn't want me to have nightmares. I took his advice and did not insist on seeing her; a decision I regret even to this day. And though I lost my father the year before, at that moment this hurt more! I cried and grieved to a point. However, when a family friend who had become a godfather to us while we were in Tuscaloosa visited us, he sympathetically encouraged me "not to cry," and I stopped!

Nonetheless, I would cry again at the death of my grandmother less than two years later. I cried once I got the news, and all the way down interstate I-65 from Montgomery to Mobile. And although Annie Mae Miller Taylor, aka my "MaMa," was my heart, the tears had to stop, because I had to take care of business. With my father being her only child, she added my name to all of her matters of business after his death. Although R.L. and M.J. were older, she entrusted me, jokingly saying, "If I put dem boys in charge, they liable to put me in a pine box and keep on going." Although she said it jokingly, her reasoning had merit.

My mother and her favorite niece helped me, but her grandsons did nothing in the way of making her final arrangements. D.W. and his wife went with me to the family viewing when they got in from Dallas, Texas, but the three grandsons who carried the Miller name might as well have "put her in a pine box and kept on going." R.L. had the audacity to complain about not being listed as the first grandson in her obituary! I dismissed him by saying, "*Boy, please!*"

Even though I was young, and this hurt like nothing I had experienced before, including the loss of my dad and Maya, I had to fold it all up, put it away in the pocket of my *Superwoman* cape, and do what had to be done. My MaMa depended on me to do so. My reluctance to cry in these and other hurtful moments has been perceived by others as a symbol of strength. Over time, I embraced it and wore it as a badge of honor. However, it was one that would eventually come with a price I could not afford to pay.

Many years later while in seminary, I was informed about the healing nature of tears by one of my Pastoral Care professors, Rev. Dr. Carolyn McCrary. Our tears taste different because they have different chemical compositions, indicative of their cause, she explained. However, regardless of the composition, tears are meant to be shed. A lesson I quickly learned when she stopped me from offering one of my classmates a tissue to dry her tears during one of our group sessions. With the release of tears, the emotions that compose or cause those tears are also released, whether hurt, anger, fear, or joy. Yet it would be sometime later before I understood the assignment.

> **REFLECTION**
>
> In hindsight, I am more appreciative of the value of the tears shed by the sinful woman in Chapter 7 of the Book of Luke, who washed Jesus's feet with her tears. Having no water to offer him as would have been the custom, the Bible says, "she stood at his feet behind him weeping, and began to wash his feet with tears and did wipe them with the hairs of her head, and kissed his feet, and anointed them with the ointment." By this expression of love, that begins with weeping, Jesus grants forgiveness of her many sins, salvation, and peace. She didn't have to stand before the church council, confess to the priest, nor tarry on a church bench as some have been taught and made to do. Just with the shedding of her tears, she released all the emotion those tears were composed of, guilt and repentance of sins, feelings of conviction, oppression, and marginalization as a result thereof, and her love and faith in her Savior.

Chapter 8
I Finally Cried!

"I never would have imagined I'd be here," I thought. I would have wagered any money I or anyone else had that I wouldn't have wound up in this situation! After all, as one of my goddaughter's put it, "Ma, he's a whole lawyer!" Despite the fact that he had been unfaithful for most if not all of our marriage, he had always been a provider. Once his career as an attorney took off, he always made sure that neither the girls nor I went lacking in any material thing we needed nor most of the things we wanted. If he could afford it or settle a case or two to earn the money, we had it! So much so that even after we divorced, we remained friends and supported each other in financial endeavors. I'd recommend him as a lawyer to friends, patients, and others seeking legal assistance. I'd allowed him and his two sons (conceived from one of his extramarital affairs) to remain on my family health insurance policy for an extended period of time after the divorce. My kindness would allow him time to find his own coverage as he requested. Likewise, he was supportive of me and our daughters and had been faithful in paying child support for the three years following the divorce until a couple of months before he remarried. I'd often brag on him to friends, colleagues, and other single mothers, saying jokingly yet earnestly, "I got a good baby daddy!"

But all of that changed, and here I was in the midst of a court battle. I never wanted to be where I found myself. To avoid being here, I'd stayed in the marriage long after it had been clearly forsaken. My mom had been in this position when my father failed to pay child support for us after he and my mom divorced. I just didn't want to go through what she went through, nor did I want my daughters to experience what I had during my childhood as a result. So, I stayed much longer than I should have. I even prayed that he'd return to doing right by us as I had requested of him when I asked for the divorce. But I know now that it was a journey I had to take not just for me, but also for my daughters and for other women who found themselves on a similar path. A journey to teach my daughters that there are times you must stand for what's right, even when it doesn't feel good. Surprisingly, it was a journey that revealed the true character of the man I married, but most importantly, a journey to restore my faith, trust, and confidence in God.

The first time I'd cried (since prior to the divorce) was not because of what one might expect. When we finalized the agreement, I didn't cry. I always assumed it was because by then, I had cried out of tears! My husband cried and my lawyer, who is also a very dear mutual friend of us both and had agreed to file the divorce settlement for us as long we were amiable, even shed tears. Not one drop did I shed until I felt the pain of a mother who could not protect her daughter from the fallout of her parents' failed marriage. I now understand that my lack of tears at the end of the marriage was not that I had exhausted my supply, but rather because my divorce was not felt as a loss but rather an act of freedom.

Among the lies he filed to the court in response to my complaint alleging his failure to pay child support for our younger daughter as agreed in the divorce settlement, was that I'd been neglectful in my duties as the custodial parent. By "leaving her in the care of multiple people while her mom was away at seminary, as if she was a vagabond," I was not fulfilling my responsibilities to her. Of course, this was the furthest thing from the truth. Now I had come to expect his lies (so much so that I'd nicknamed him "lie-awyer" as opposed to lawyer), but this one hurt like none other! And finally, I cried.

Everyone who knows me, knows how dear I hold the gift of my daughters and how serious I am about my duties as a mother, especially him. I have text messages and cards he had given me bestowing accolades and expressing his gratitude for the exceptional mother I am to our daughters. As recently as months before I filed a complaint concerning his delinquency in child support, he'd given me "big ups" for being a great mother. Now he was scandalizing my name and honor as a mother.

I realize the tears came from much deeper sources than his lies. Now, I cried the tears that I had not cried when my father died some thirty years prior. Not one tear had I shed for the loss of the man I called "Daddy" and of whom I thought the world as a little girl until now. This nearly identical unjustified betrayal and desertion by the other man I trusted to love, protect, and provide for me and my children, that I experienced by my father, opened the floodgates of my pent-up pain, and I finally cried. For my daughter because I knew that pain of having a father who failed to support you financially, I cried. For my mom because as a mother I felt the hurt she must have felt, I cried. For *me* because I had trusted him and he had betrayed that trust in *every way*, I finally cried!

When I couldn't trust him to be faithful to our marriage, nor as a companion, nor as a lover, I trusted him to be a provider for our children. It was the only hope in him I had left and the only validation that I hadn't totally misjudged him as a person. I realized I had done just that, and I mourned with heavy tears. His actions and the never-ending lies obliterated that trust and the validity of the character I had envisioned all those years ago! If he were Pinocchio, his nose would have been on the floor! As a friend of mine once said, there was "no level of unrighteousness it appeared he wasn't willing to stoop."

Yet, if I had to do it all over again, not having the benefit of hindsight or the wisdom I have now, I would! It was the hand life dealt me, and I had *no choice* but to play the hand as I saw it, even though it didn't play out the way I thought it would. To play it any differently would have negated any wins or blessings I gained in the process, the greatest being the two amazing daughters God blessed me with during the marriage.

I'm reminded of being hesitant to name our youngest daughter as we did, because it was so close in spelling to her father's name that I feared people would think I named her after him, like Black folk often do! Lol! He certainly wasn't deserving of that honor, but I'm so glad I didn't listen to that spirit of damnation within, because she has been all of the "strength, grace, and promise of God" her name stands for. It took some soul searching, counseling sessions, and much prayer to arrive at this place of peace within. Along the way, I questioned whether I had done the best thing for my child, and even condemned myself for trusting him. But the Bible teaches us in I John 3:20 that even when "our hearts condemn us, God is greater than our hearts and knows all things."

INSIGHT

There are times when the strength of your *superpower* comes through moral and ethical stances or just doing what you know is right, even if it's not popular or doesn't feel good while doing it. We must not feel guilty or condemned for doing so.

Prayer Of Restoration

Most gracious and merciful God, our Great Redeemer, who is able to pick us up out of the deepest pits of despair, and place our feet on solid ground that we may walk in the way you have laid for us, I offer this prayer on behalf of all of your children, who are broken in spirit and in heart by the pain of betrayal, that you will restore them and make them whole again, as only you can. Heal their broken hearts and bandage up their wounds, so that the pain they feel will hurt no more. Help them, Oh Lord, to find strength and comfort in their faith and confidence in you, trusting and believing that while they have been betrayed by others, who they loved and trusted, you will never leave nor forsake them. Give them a spirit of love, power, and a sound mind that they will be fearful nor weary of anyone or anything. In Jesus's name, I pray. Amen.

Chapter 9
My Lying Heart

Did she just take a gun from under that pillow? Surely my eyes are lying to me, I thought. But it was not my eyes that were lying to me but *my heart*! It was my heart that said I didn't really see what I saw, or what I saw didn't look like what it was. She, who I refer to as "J.Z.B." was my next-door neighbor. She and her mother appeared as typical neighbors.

They were more than cordial to us—my then husband and me—chatting often as we passed each other outside of our townhouse apartments. We invited them to gatherings hosted at our home, like for my birthday. As my third pregnancy progressed, they would even bring food over when they cooked or from the restaurant the mother owned "to make sure the baby I was carrying in my belly was well-fed," the mother usually said.

But then my perspective began to change. I wondered why the two of them needed a housekeeper for a two-bedroom apartment, and when the mother asked my husband how many million-dollar cases he had won, both of my eyebrows raised. He and I laughed because at the time he was barely out of law school and was only making a little more than my salary at the time, about $31,000 yearly. I didn't make much of it, because I wasn't trying to be best friends with either of them.

It would have been wise to note that other females obviously didn't care to be friends with J.Z.B. either, or vice versa! Because every sister girl has girlfriends, right? At least a few who you could confide in, choose to be the maid/matron of honor of your wedding, and/or the godmother of your children, right? This should especially be the case if a sister still lives in the town where she was born, reared, and graduated high school, right? Well, I've met a few women in my life who proved themselves to be untrustworthy as a sister or girlfriend. This is what I would learn of J.Z.B.

My suspicions grew as I noticed the increasing amount of time my husband was spending with J.Z.B. For example, when he got home from work, instead of coming in to eat dinner with me before I left for my night shift at the hospital as he usually did, he would stop at their house. After we moved into our new home, he continued to visit multiple times "to drop off this or that to her mother," so he said. The tell all was when he went to help them move J.Z.B.'s sister in the week after Guardian Angel was born! He barely lifted a finger at our home, and now he was lifting furniture and such! Really? I expressed my suspicion to my mother and childhood BFF, who were staying with me for a few days to help with the baby as I recovered from having a C-section.

Several weeks later, on a Friday evening, those suspicions unfolded into truth. Normally we would have gone out to dinner, but he called and said he was at a lawyer association's dinner. My suspicion intensified because I'd been to several of those events, and the background noise didn't sound like that was the case. I decided to drive downtown to where he said he was to see if he was telling the truth. As I drove, a voice from within told me to ride by J.Z.B.'s apartment first. I listened and when I arrived, his car was parked outside of their apartment, but her car was not there! When her mother finally came to the door after I rang the doorbell repeatedly, I asked for him. She said he wasn't there. I asked for J.Z.B. She claimed she didn't know where she was. I expressed my concerns about the amount of time J.Z.B. and my husband were spending together and didn't reserve any words by doing so! I didn't curse at her, but I made my discontent concerning the matter quite clear! I was not a minister then by any meaning of the word. But this experience would later be a testimony that ministers to others.

The mother tried to justify the time that her daughter and my husband were spending together by saying, "Oh, they don't be doing nothing but talking and drinking that dark funny-tasting beer." Although I was married at the time, when it came to matters of the heart and relationships, I was young, dumb, and quite naïve. I saw and heard the truth, but my heart wanted to believe her lie. Besides, what kind of mother allows her daughter to entertain a married man in her home, and a married man with a newborn baby at that? What kind of mother would aid and abet her daughter in such disgraceful wrongdoing? He wouldn't have gotten past the front doorsteps at Alice T. Miller's house! Period!

Meanwhile, I made several calls to my husband and made him very aware of where I was and where he was not, and that I would be waiting outside of their apartment until he returns. Several minutes later, he walked up the sidewalk—but still no J.Z.B. He lied and said he was at a Muslim worship service that was being held at that apartment complex's clubhouse, and that he didn't invite me because he knew I wouldn't go. That much was true, but everything else was a big fat lie! He later admitted that he was having dinner with J.Z.B., and she had dropped him at the entrance of the complex to avoid confrontation with me.

I finally felt the need to stop speculating and talk with J.Z.B. myself. I called her home phone before I went to make sure she was there but didn't say anything. I didn't want her to leave before I got there or have some prepared response to what she thought I would say. She already knew and was expecting me. And oh, was she prepared, loaded, cocked, and ready to aim and shoot if I had stepped to her in the wrong way!

But what she prepared for is not how I approached her. At this point, I just wanted to talk woman to woman concerning my husband. He had several platonic friendships with females, and in my heart, I wanted this to be the same. The difference is those platonic girlfriends of his usually became my friends too, but J.Z.B. never did. This I noted to be so when she didn't come to the gathering my husband hosted to celebrate our new home and Guardian Angel's birth.

No, ma'am! No, sir! She was no friend of mine but rather my enemy! She threw up this smoke screen, suggesting my husband wasn't the kind of man who would cheat, that he was more of a nerdy type of guy, expounding on his so-called "nerdiness!" She must have been such a lover of cheating "nerds" that she wanted to establish a legacy of such. Eventually, she not only conceived one child from her affair with that "nerd," but two!

When it was clear that I didn't come to be confrontational as she thought I would because her mother told her how upset I was before, J.Z.B. then takes a loaded gun from under one of the sofa's throw pillows, uncocks it, and places it on the counter in plain sight for my *eyes* to see! All the while, she smiled and made small talk with me concerning those things a girlfriend would talk about.

What had my lying heart gotten me into? My lying heart that said it may not be what it looked like. My lying heart that wouldn't let me feel the hurt of being betrayed by my husband. I was obviously out of my league! This was deceit on a whole other level, beyond that of Delilah or even Jezebel. This was dangerous deceit. If the gun was to protect her, why take it out when it was clear that I meant her no harm? The eeriness I now feel as I write this, I don't recall feeling then. I don't even recall being scared as I leisurely walked out, drove to my friend's house, picked up my baby, and went home.

It's like when my car crashed into the freeway barrier! I possibly realized how close I came to death and still somehow kept my wits about me. But now I cringe at the thought . . . I was in her house. She had every right to defend herself as it surely would have been said, had she shot and killed me. And she would have been raising my baby daughter. But the *grace* of *God*!

INSIGHT

This is the case where I could have chosen wiser. Whether I chose to stay in the marriage or leave, I really didn't need to talk to her, and definitely not at her home! I didn't need to show her that I was his wife; she already knew that. And I knew the truth concerning them, but my heart chose not to believe it because the truth hurt too bad! Knowing the truth about them also revealed the truth about me and my vulnerability. I discerned the truth concerning J.Z.B.'s and her mother's intentions years before this happened, and I dismissed the significance of that revelation. Yet, more importantly, the Spirit of the Lord redirected my path and guided me to the truth concerning my husband that evening, but I was not ready to handle the truth!

We must not ignore the truth nor believe the enemy's lies even when our hearts lead us to. The Bible teaches us that as Jesus prepared His Disciples for His departure, He said to them, "**I still have many things to say to you, but you cannot bear them now . . . but when the Spirit of truth comes, he will *guide* you into *all* the truth . . . (John 16:12–13).**" Thus, when God speaks *truth* to us through the Spirit, He has already prepared a way for us to endure it. We must trust the Holy Spirit to be:

1. Our *guide* that reveals/leads us to the *truth*—we must listen and obey.
2. Our *comforter* to console our hearts and minds that we may see and accept the reality of the *truth*—we must not allow the pain of the truth to question its reality.
3. Our *advocate* that makes intercession for us through prayer that will help us in our weakness to overcome the challenges the *truth* may present—we must seek the help of the Spirit through prayer! Scripture tells us that "Even when we do not know what to say or pray, the Holy Spirit makes intercessions for us through groaning that cannot be uttered in words" (Romans 8:28).

Chapter 10
The Makings for a Rainbow

"Mommy, whose little white baby is this?" my Guardian Angel asked as she placed the newborn photo before my eyes. "I asked Daddy, but he wouldn't tell me!" she explained further. The one thing I asked of him when he confirmed the rumors that he had fathered a baby outside of our marriage was not to tell our five-year-old daughter yet. Give me some time to digest this first, I pleaded. I didn't even know what I was going to do at that time: pack up my child and go home to my momma or stay and ride this storm out too.

That should not have been too much to ask, you would think! Yet he failed to do even that! I felt like I had been sucker punched in my stomach! I had been walking around feeling numb and void since the night he admitted it to me. The pain of the tooth I had pulled earlier the same day no longer hurt, but I felt the pain of this now. The heartache, anger, shock, betrayal, embarrassment, fear, all of it I felt with one look at that baby! I felt it and I expressed it!

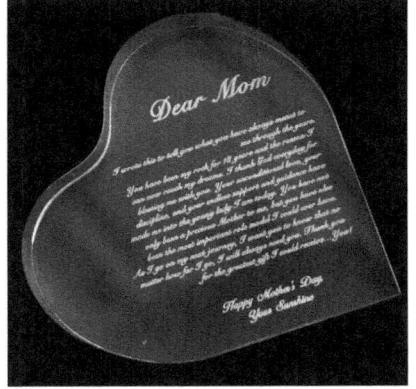

I let him have it verbally but physically took my pain out on his office furniture! He claimed that he had shown the photo to Pamela and her husband, Gregory, close family friends who came over from Georgia to be supportive earlier that day, and had placed it in his top desk drawer. Later, while he was on a business call, our daughter took it out before he realized it. I asked our friends to watch my daughter and left the office.

I met up with Marie who was and still is a faithful and trustworthy friend in every sense of the word. She had been there through the good and the bad since we moved to Montgomery and was by my side through this storm as well. Sometime later, our family friends called me and pleaded with me to join them for dinner. We met at our favorite Thai restaurant. Pamela and Gregory urged the waiter to make the drink I ordered as strong as possible, as if it could numb my pain. It did not! It hurt just the same, but life must go on! Right? It had continued through every other traumatic event in my life. As life went on, I contemplated leaving daily and rehearsed the steps of how I would do it.

It made sense to return home to Mobile because I would have the help of my mother, childhood BFF, Annick, and other family members to help with my child. Then I imagined how I would feel when it was time for my child to visit her father in Montgomery, and I became nauseated at the thought. Meanwhile, I began to hear a familiar theme in the advice I received from others, some from folk I respected and some from those I would have never consulted on the matter. Regardless of the source, the advice seemed to be sending the same message as the chorus of a song, and that was to stay or at least that I shouldn't feel like I must leave then, as with my GSM (God-Sent Mother), who advised me to "just walk slow and pray!"

Based on social and cultural norms that condone the promiscuous behaviors of men, married or not, some encouraged me to stay. "Men will be men… or he's still young, he'll come in after while," they rationalized. These responses were not surprising. My grandmother also tried to justify my father's infidelity by saying that my dad was coming back home if my mom had not filed for a divorce. However, I was surprised when my forever father-in-love did an about-face in his response! Initially, he was very consoling and empathetic and assured me I would always be in his family regardless of whether his son and I were together. The next day when he called, his tone turned defiant and indignant concerning the matter, as he encouraged me to stay if I could, explaining that he'd been thinking about how I supported his son through law school, and that I should be the one that benefits from his son's inevitable success as a lawyer, not J.Z.B!

I really didn't know what to make of his advice, but it was just the beginning of a tidal wave of unexpected and even jaw-dropping advice. My eyebrow was raised when a friend from work, of whom she and my former husband had no love lost between them said, "Coretta, I can't tell you whether to stay or leave … I ain't got but a room and a broom, but if you decide to leave, you and baby girl welcome to it." I was expecting her to say something like, "You need to leave that n****r and take him to the cleaners," but in that moment she didn't. Likewise, I became speechless by my BFF's response! Surely, she would say while on her way to help me, "Get your child, pack your sh*t, and come home," but instead she encouraged me not to leave MY home!" Yet, I would still be amazed.

Shortly thereafter, during a visit to Florida, one of his older brothers came to the car that I was sitting in and abruptly began to encourage me to hang in there, saying, "Her trick not gone work." He was always nice to me and supportive of the marriage as a whole, but I really didn't think it mattered that much to him. I was pleasantly surprised that it did. Yet the advice from a friendly acquaintance who had experienced the same situation, not as the wife but the mistress who had a baby by a married man, was mind blowing! Not only did she encourage me to stay but urged me to have another baby! What was God saying to me?

That message soon became clear one day during a marriage counseling session. Initially, we were making progress. Our counselor was a conservative-looking Caucasian female who operated in a way nothing like her appearance. She challenged him on his self-righteous claims, saying in one of the first sessions, "I don't give a damn if you are a rising lawyer, you should consider yourself lucky your wife is even willing to try and make the marriage work!" But she began to meet resistance from him when she led each of us individually to examine ourselves introspectively. I was offended when she asked him to make a list of ways his affair made the marriage better. WTH was she talking about, I wondered? Later I understood that the purpose of the assignment was to realize that in the two of us, he had the perfect wife, or to make it plain: the mistress added the 20 percent to the 80 percent that the wife had given, which makes 100.

It was an assignment that he never completed nor even gave a legitimate effort. Feeling frustrated during one of our sessions, I asked our therapist to begin divorce counseling with our daughter and abruptly left the room. As I walked past my daughter, who was busy in another room coloring in a book our therapist gave her, she said to me, "Momma, that ain't nothing but the devil, but he won't win!" Frozen in my steps, I thought, "Jesus, what is this five-year-old little girl saying?" This was the first of many prophetic statements (beyond her age and knowledge) spoken to me through her, from which I nicknamed her "Guardian Angel." I gathered myself, continued out the door, and left with Marie, whom I had called and asked to come pick me up.

There would be a time to leave, but it was clear that this wasn't it. I don't know whether time healed my wound, or I just grew numb to the pain as I had done in so many other instances, but eventually the hours of that horrific evening turned to days, days to weeks, and weeks to months, months to a year or more, and I was still in the marriage! Then it happened. The thing I feared from the moment I learned of him. If it were painful to just see him in a photo, I dreaded what experiencing him walk, run, talk, laugh, or cry would feel like. It was nothing like I feared!

As he ran down the hallway behind Guardian Angel toward her room, I felt the same as I feel with all children, nothing but pure joy! He was somewhere between 15 to 18 months old, and he was wearing a yellow cotton shorts romper with a white Peter Pan collar, just like I would have dressed my boy if I had one. It didn't matter who his mother was, or what she and his father had done to me. I fell in love with PP (for Peter Pan-collared little boy) just like I had with the nephew of a friend of ours.

Meanwhile, things between his father and me stayed the same. I focused on raising my daughter and soon thereafter returned to school to become a nurse practitioner. That dream of being a pediatrician began to yearn within while I was working as a school nurse. Having a young daughter and an unstable marriage, I decided to become a pediatric nurse practitioner instead. I would not make as much money, but I would be able to do most of what doctors do.

Within a few months of beginning the EARN Nursing program at Auburn University in Montgomery, an expedited bridge program designed to allow registered nurses with associate degrees to earn a bachelor's degree in one year, I learned that I was pregnant! During the time my father-in-law was ill, we grew close again. I knew exactly when the baby was conceived and didn't regret the pregnancy at all! I continued in the program and excelled at it! My *Superwoman* cape had regained its strength! A friend questioned how I could make an *A* on my assignments amid what I was going through, and I replied by saying, "In this I have some control in the outcome; if I study hard enough, I'll do well."

I flourished in that strength, and then six months before I graduated, *my sunshine* came bursting through the rain! She was "the prettiest baby in the nursery," the nurses told her dad and my mom! Of course, I had wished for a boy the moment I learned I was pregnant and had ignored the results of the ultrasound that predicted a girl, waited until the very last month to design the nursery, and even then, chose the unisex color yellow just in case! I accepted and grew to love PP, but I wanted my own BOY! That changed the moment I saw my baby girl, and I repented of all of that!

Yet no sooner than I experienced the sunshine, the rain reappeared. While battling the stabbing gas pains that came with the C-section delivery, I was sucker punched again, because I didn't see it coming. After examining my newborn baby, the pediatrician walked into my room, introduced herself, and asked me, "Are you PP's mother too?" In the midst of my sunny days, I'd forgotten that of all the pediatricians in our city, his mother had chosen the exact same practice that my Guardian Angel went to. My daughter's pediatrician and one of the other partners of the practice knew of the situation, and never would have said that, but this was one of the newer doctors making weekend rounds, and she did not know. I simply replied, "no," but the gas pains suddenly felt ten times worse than before!

Nevertheless, the joy of my new baby girl, who I would later affectionately call *my sunshine*, overcame all of that! I gave her the name "Sunshine" because each morning that I went into the nursery to get her out of the crib, she would always be full of *joy*! I took an extended maternity leave, graduated with my bachelor's degree in May 2003, and began my master's program at the University of South Alabama three months later. It was mostly online, which enabled me to complete my studies and keep my baby girl out of daycare during the first two years of her life. I returned to work but only on a part-time basis to keep my license active, and my neighbor usually kept my baby then and when I had to complete my clinical internship.

Despite learning that the man I was married to had fathered yet another son by the same woman, less than a year before finishing the program, I graduated and became a Certified Pediatric Nurse Practitioner. The next few years were filled with separations and reconciliations, but some people within the community didn't know, because in some ways we behaved as a normal family, like going on vacation with the kids together. We even benefited from a marriage repair workshop that a friend recommended.

Finally, the sun was shining on our marriage, it seemed. We were able to buy our forever home. After falling in love with it, we had a little initial difficulty with financing, but I heard the voice of the Lord say as with the prophet Jeremiah (29:11) "For I know the plans I have for you . . . to prosper you and not to harm you, plans to give you hope and a future." We were able to move forward with purchasing the house at a great price. Everything in the home I dreamed of and wrote about in my journal and had been convinced I would have to build to get everything I wanted. But God had given me my heart's desire in this home, down to the slate tiled floor on the screened porch, and it was turnkey. I searched high and low for just the right furnishings to design it just the way I imagined the first time I walked through the doors. I even found joy in designing the boys' room as I would if I had given birth to them. Life was very doable.

> **INSIGHT**
>
> Just as a *rainbow* is formed as light slowly travels through a raindrop, bending and separating into wavelengths of color that are reflected off the inside of the raindrop, we can still experience moments of joy and happiness in the midst of painful and troubling times. We just have to hold steadfast to the promises of God. Oftentimes women have asked how I came to accept his two sons, while admitting that they may have dealt with the cheating, but not the children. Yet it wasn't any effort on my part, but rather the "the *joy* of the *lord* that was my strength" (Nehemiah 8:10). As I lived through these and other storms in my marriage, God also allowed me to experience seasons of joy and happiness and witness the fulfillment of His promises.

Chapter 11
A Taste of Glory

"Go back and try the one on display at the end of the counter," I heard the Spirit say. I was about to leave one of my favorite local beauty supply stores feeling defeated and dejected. For nearly an hour, I tried on numerous wigs, but I could not find one that did not look like a wig! As a child, I teased my "MaMa" about wearing wigs, and here I was having to wear the same. I was younger than my grandma when she started wearing wigs, but when I looked in the mirror, I saw her. I felt defeated because for many years I had been able to hide my hair loss, and now I was about to be exposed!

I first noticed the dime-sized bald spot at the crown of my scalp around age twenty-two, which was about six months before I got married. My hairdresser at that time passed it off as a nervous spot and cautioned me against scratching or picking at that area. But the area slowly became larger, so I visited a dermatologist in Tuscaloosa, Alabama, where we were living at the time. He diagnosed it as alopecia but offered no real solution—just told me not to perm, braid, press, or hot iron my hair, which as a Black woman left me with no logical hair style options.

For a few years I got by with hairstyles that covered the bald spot. But after the birth of our first child, it became significantly worse to the point that it became difficult to hide unless I wore my hair pulled back in a bun or ponytail, which was not attractive to me. I explored treatments prescribed by a local African American male dermatologist that involved a biopsy of my scalp for scientific study along with injections and ointments, but had little success, if any. Several years later when I became a nurse practitioner, I learned of an African American female dermatologist who practiced in Birmingham, Alabama. She had some success with some newer treatments in reducing the inflammation and slowing the process down some, but no regrowth of hair.

Meanwhile, a friend introduced me to a hairdresser that designed very natural-looking hairstyles using hair extensions. I always used 100 percent human hair that was identical in color to my natural hair, and blended in so perfectly that many people didn't know I was wearing weaved hair nor had any idea that I had extensive alopecia. While wearing the "tree braids," the grandmother of one of my patients thought I was kin to a family she had known for years because she thought I had the "same good hair" for which they were known. I laughed and thanked her for her kindness, but I didn't tell her that it wasn't all my natural hair.

Tree braiding involves interweaving loose hair extensions into my braided hair in a way that looks like the limbs of a tree. However, with my hair becoming thinner and made worse by the added tension on the hair involved with tree braiding, we had to stop. We then began what is called a sew-in. We only added tracts to the area that was missing hair at first, but eventually as my edges became worn, we did a complete sew-in. Regardless of whether it was a partial or full sew-in, my stylist always did an excellent job that looked natural, which was very important to me. Many people didn't know the difference. One of my sorority sisters asked me after I had just gotten my hair done what I used to get my hair to grow so healthy and full of body!

    These compliments were a common occurrence. On this occasion and over time, I usually revealed that it was a sew-in. I would even share the type and brand of hair I used and where I bought it. This usually upset my mom if she was with me. She would insist that I should not tell them! For me this was a compliment as I explained to a church sister who after admiring my haircut from afar, became shameful and apologetic when I revealed to her that it wasn't all my hair. To be honest, I felt a sense of pride that I had been able to overcome another weakness. But it wasn't my glory to claim, as I learned years later when my new dermatologist recommended I stop the sew-ins and wear wigs instead. So that day, after not being able to find a wig that didn't look like a wig, I left the store feeling dejected and low in spirit as if someone had let the air out of me. The hope I had when I left my new dermatologist's office was now gone.

    As an African American female, she could relate to the challenges my condition presented for me and offered practical treatment options, unlike the first dermatologist, who happened to be a Caucasian male. I was hopeful because she was the first dermatologist in more than twenty years to finally diagnose my condition accurately: Central Centrifugal Cicatricial Alopecia (CCCA). CCCA is the most common type of scarring hair loss for women of African descent and runs in families. With the diagnosis, she presented several contemporary treatment options, and even though the maximum expected hair regrowth is only 30 percent, I looked forward to it. Just maybe I would be able to wear my natural hair again someday.

As I made my way out the door of the beauty supply store, I panicked! What was I going to do? I had to go to work the next day! I had been revealing to people that I wore weaved hairstyles, but I hadn't told them that I had alopecia. In my panic, I lost reasoning that would have reminded me that wearing wigs was a current fashion trend. Even women who have full heads of hair wore wigs. But that wisdom escaped me in that moment because I was more concerned about people finding out I had alopecia! What people saw as an asset in me would now be seen as a flaw or weakness the same way my mom obviously did. Why else would she not want me to share with others that I was wearing a weave?

But my panic went beyond that. Not only had I seen my grandmother in the mirror as I tried on various wigs, but I recalled seeing an older cousin's scalp when my Mama and I visited her at the nursing home a few years prior. She was my grandma's favorite niece and experienced hair loss also. I had not lost as much hair as she had at that time, but I could clearly see the same pattern of loss in her scalp as I had. I was horrified at what was to come. I didn't deal with it then nor had I really dealt with it in the years prior. I felt vulnerable and broken when the weave was out, especially when others were at the hairdresser during the same time. But as soon as my stylist completed my hair, I felt whole again. All those years, I carried the burden that the world places on women and girls to be "perfect" in appearance. For years, my daughters didn't know the extent of my hair loss because I hid it from them.

I had not been taught in all of our churchgoing that I was "fearfully and wonderfully made," and God didn't make a mistake in creating the "white-girl-shaped body" I was teased and scorned for having in my teen and young adult years. But rather, that "my frame was not hidden from Him when I was made in the secret place and was woven together in the depths of the earth," as David proclaims in Psalm 139. And that "(His) eyes saw my unformed body; all the days ordained for me were written in (His) book before one of them came to be!" Maybe if I had, I wouldn't have cursed my body well into my late thirties, stopping only when I realized that my teen daughter was doing the same. But I hadn't been and so I cursed the shape of my body, its size, knocked knees, short toes, long head, huge breasts and anything I thought was not perfect or pretty enough. I cursed the hell out of this damned *alopecia* because while I couldn't change many of the aforementioned imperfections, once I was able to afford it, my hair was always on point!

There was a lesson to learn in my journey. As I transitioned from tree braids to partial sew-ins to full sew-ins to wigs and beyond, there was always one common factor: I was wearing it! As for the wig that the Spirit told me to go back and try—it was perfect! Or at least it would be as soon as my stylist cut it in the layered hairstyle I usually wore. I returned to work the next day, and no one knew any difference. God had done it again!

Years later another church sister asked me what I did to make my wigs not look like wigs, unlike the way she felt hers looked. If only I had seen myself in that mirror through the lens God does! I shared some of my tips with her, but I've come to learn that it's never really been about the wigs, nor the stylist, or even the person wearing it, but rather the glory of God that shines through them. A glory that would be present even if the person happened to be bald. For that reason, I name *all* my wigs "*Glory*" to acknowledge the beauty and magnificence of God that shines through them on *me*! And if I decide to wear my head bald, she shall be called the same.

> **INSIGHT**
>
> So often, we fail to see the *beauty* of God revealed within us, because we only see beauty as that defined by the world, which is usually based on physical appearances, and the material and cosmetic coverings we wear on them. Even when we do not see what God sees in us, others do. I am mindful of one day when we were in our early twenties, my BFF, Annick, looked me in the eyes and said, "You are so pretty . . . I've always thought so!" Throughout our childhood, I longed for the slim body frame she had and all the trendy hairstyles and fashions that her family could afford to give her, but mine could not. While all along, she thought I was already pretty as I was! When it comes to our physical appearance, we must have confidence that if God was pleased when he created us the way we are (Genesis 1:31), then, regardless of what cosmetic or material coverings we may add to it, *we in ourselves are enough!*

Chapter 12
This Cape Doesn't Fit Anymore!

My pastor asked during a session of spiritual counseling, *"What is staying doing to you?"* I couldn't answer because I had given it no thought. So, I said, "I'll get back with you." To examine my motive for staying, I had to reflect on my whole life to that point. This is what I saw. I knew what staying did for my daughters, or at least I thought. It would protect their financial well-being and ensure that their college education would be paid for without the struggle I had experienced and prevent them from delaying or compromising their dreams as I had done.

Since I was a young child, I'd been told that I always talked about becoming a pediatrician, "a doctor that takes care of kids." But as a divorced, single parent struggling to provide for five children on a maid's salary, and with practically no child support from my father since they'd divorced when I was ten years old, I understood that there was no way my mom could afford to put me through medical school. Instead of pursuing a career as a pediatrician, I settled for pediatric nursing. I graduated with an Associate Degree in Nursing, became a registered nurse by twenty years of age, and worked for two years on the pediatric unit at Mobile Infirmary Hospital until I married in November

1990 and moved to Tuscaloosa, Alabama, where my husband at the time was enrolled in law school.

For the next twenty years, I wore the *Superwoman cape* proudly! I wore it as the sole provider and home manager of our household while my husband was in law school at the University of Alabama. He had explained that it would be very difficult for him to work and perform well in school, thus there was no bridging the gap with any consistent part-time work on his part. Except for the funds from a summer internship and a student loan that he was eventually able to get once he became a permanent resident of the United States, my income from working as an RN at Bryce Hospital, a long-term mental health facility in the city, provided the sole income to maintain our household and standard of living.

This meant we pretty much lived check-to-check. The stark reality of our financial situation was made vividly clear when an error was made in my payroll leaving me with only $1.09 in the bank instead of the usual $1,000 or so. We were initially told it could be a week or more before it was corrected. Because I was the sole provider, our livelihood was instantly threatened. Not only were the checks for the bills we had just put in the mail on the way to work that day invalid, but the money for food, gas, rent, personal needs, and everything we depended upon my payroll to provide was not accessible. We had to go all the way to the CEO's office to resolve the issue, but they had an emergency paycheck prepared and ready for me the next day.

By the time I became a mother with the birth of our oldest daughter in July 1995, I was comfortable wearing the superwoman cape. My mother had worn it working tirelessly within and outside of our home as head of household to provide our needs after she and my father divorced. I came to understand this as her expression of love for us. So, to express love for my children, it felt natural to go above and beyond as their mother and primary caregiver to not only provide their daily needs, but also to insure their well-being. I worked the night shift the first two years of Guardian Angel's life to ensure she didn't have to go to daycare, because I knew with my experience in pediatric nursing that babies become sicker more frequently when they are in daycare. I also used much of my paid leave from work to chaperone my children's field trips and attend most of their school activities. In fact, Guardian Angel didn't go on her first field trip without me until her eighth-grade class went to Washington, DC. The only reason was because her father was unavailable to go, and I just couldn't bring myself to leave Sunshine, who was only a preschooler at the time. I remember Guardian Angel saying, "Mom, you've taught me for thirteen years now. I'll be alright."

These accounts and countless others are given not to diminish the presence of their father in their lives, but rather to draw a pattern of the supermom cape I wore at that time, and the weight it carried. My reluctance to leave the marriage ultimately had been to protect their emotional and material well-being. Sunshine said it best when, at the age of three or four, she returned home from an outing with her father to find that I wasn't there. I went on a girl's day outing with a friend, and when I returned, Sunshine shook her little finger toward me and scolded me saying, "Mommy, when I left to go with Daddy, you were here, but when I got home, you were not here," because I had always been there! This supermom role I fully embraced without apology, all while maintaining a full-time job and contributing to the expense of the lifestyle we lived, except when I was on maternity leave or in school. Even then I contributed through paid leave and/or part-time jobs, like I did while pursuing my Master of Nursing degree.

I had also embraced the superwoman role as a committed wife in a marriage to a grossly unfaithful husband. At first, I stayed out of fear because once his suspected infidelity was confirmed by the birth of the first of two sons born out of the adulterous affair with J.Z.B., I had both legal and Biblical justification for leaving; yet I stayed. I feared the unknown and the known. I didn't know what life as a single parent would be like for me and my oldest daughter, but I had an idea based on what my mom and other single moms I knew had gone through. I didn't know what it would be like for us, and that scared me. I did, however, know what it was like for me as a child of a single mom. I feared that for my child also. So, I didn't make a choice to leave. I chose to stay.

I remembered I had stayed through multiple separations and many attempts to reconcile our marriage, through counseling sessions, and much prayer. I stayed through the birth of our second daughter, our first daughter's high school graduation, and what was supposed to be our forever home. I reflected on how I had persevered through two additional degrees, yet I stayed. I stayed through many people advising me to stay and when some questioned why I didn't leave.

I stayed beyond my desire to be married to him and after I was no longer in love with him. I stayed years after I no longer cared for him to even touch me, especially after I learned he had been unfaithful again. After ending the affair with the mother of his sons, I learned he had been having an affair for years with yet another woman. One Saturday morning after staying out the night before, he gave me his wallet so I could pay a friend for doing our youngest daughter's hair. Unbeknownst to him, the woman he laid with the night before had written her name with a Sharpie pen next to his name in the fold of his wallet! I responded by saying to let her know that I had received her message, and though I ended all forms of intimacy between us from that day on, I stayed. I stayed through our first daughter's high school graduation and her first semester of college.

Meanwhile, the cape kept getting bigger and bigger until it became too large for me. I had been swallowed up in it like a little girl when she tries on her mother's dress or high-heeled shoes. So, when my pastor asked me, "*What was staying doing for you,*" I didn't have an answer. But it was a question I would have to answer. After taking the time to listen to my heart, something I hadn't done since I learned he had been unfaithful again, I knew I *wanted out*! Our youngest daughter had perceived within the previous two years or so that our marriage was not like that of her friends' parents. She once asked, "Mama, why I don't see you and Dad kissing and holding hands like other married people?" Having discerned even in her young mind that we were estranged, she was persistent in doing everything she could to get us back together. I knew I wanted out, but I wasn't exactly doing anything to get out! I had put the Supermom cape back on.

Our oldest daughter had a different vision. During a casual kitchen conversation, she spoke of how, shall we say, "appealing" the father of one of her male friends was. She said, "See, Mom! That's the kind of man I want you to have!" Realizing what she'd actually said, she added a caveat, "Of course, if you ever were to divorce Dad!" I was floored! What was my teenage daughter saying to me? I was so troubled by it that I consulted with my pastor the first chance I got.

She asked, *"What's your daughter about to do, Sis?"* We concluded that with her heading off to college at Hampton University, she was just trying to look out for my well-being and understood that it was not being married to her father! This I'm certain of because when I informed her the week before she left that by the time she comes home for the holidays, I would have divorced her father or at least started the process, her response was, "Good. I've been waiting on it!"

My Supermom cape had gotten too large for me to wear because, although I was willing to sacrifice my happiness and stay at least until my youngest daughter graduated high school, I had inadvertently passed it along to my daughter. I was used to my Guardian Angel speaking from a prophetic tone concerning my well-being, but never ever was it to infer that she was emotionally or physically responsible for my well-being. I met with their father in October of 2013 and asked him for two things: continue to provide the financial support to us as he had been doing and to set me free. I was legally married to him, but for several years had been living as a single woman does. I had ended all forms of intimacy with him once I learned of his latest affair. God had protected me through numerous years of his infidelity from being infected with HIV or other serious STDs, and I wasn't going to forsake His Grace anymore by risking my health. Yet I was still bound by legal obligations of marriage and, more importantly to me, what God expected of me as a wife.

Even though we were estranged and living separately for the last two to three years of the marriage, he had been faithful in being the major financial provider of our household, and along with my salary as a nurse practitioner, we and our daughters lived well. There was no reason to question his ability to provide to the extent he had been or close to it because from the moment his mistress birthed their first son, she had not worked, and he had been their major if not sole financial provider. To provide the child support that we agreed upon in the divorce settlement should not have been a hardship.

For several years after the divorce, that was the case. There was no animosity. We negotiated the terms of our divorce settlement and a very dear attorney friend of ours filed it in court for us. We remained friends and supported each other, so much so that I often bragged about how good "my baby daddy was!" The divorce was private, and its details were sealed from the public to protect his confidentiality as an attorney; many folks didn't even know that we were divorced. My superwoman cape wore well during those times. I was free to live my life as a single woman without the legal and moral obligations of being in a marriage void of matrimonial merit. I had even negotiated post-minority support for our daughters in the divorce to help provide for their college expenses. He agreed and was faithful in fulfilling his obligations. Both of our children were being well provided for by their father . . .

That all changed about three years after the divorce, when my former husband remarried. His new wife had no problem with him financially supporting her and her daughters at least six years of their adulterous affair while we were still married, but she had a problem with him fulfilling his child support obligations to our youngest daughter. He had married a woman he couldn't afford, and he began to slack on his child support payments for our minor child. Late payments turned into partial and some months none at all.

When I could no longer maneuver my finances without accumulating debt, I reluctantly consulted with a lawyer. I was hesitant because as I shared with a friend who wondered why I wouldn't do what I knew I should do, I had been here before.

My father was negligent in paying child support, and whereas my mom won the judgment, she never got the money. My friend replied by asking, where is the favor of God in that kinda thinking? Therein lies the lesson.

I had taken on the responsibility and the weight it carried of ensuring that my children would be provided for without the struggle I experienced and trusted their father to be a resource to help me do so. But it was never my burden to carry—it was God's! Just as the mother's dress looks good in the mirror to the little girl trying it on, but is impractical to wear, likewise my supermom cape no longer fit.

What my lawyer and I thought would be a quick fix turned into a four-year battle. Surely, if he wanted the divorce sealed from the public to protect his professional reputation, he would readily settle this dispute, at least I thought. But this was his domain, and he used every legal and illegal, whether moral or immoral, derogatory, and, at times, outright blasphemous tactic, to delay, deter, and nullify my claim. Finally, after two years of countless motions, pointless depositions, and costly trips to Huntsville, Alabama, the favor of God showed up in the Madison County Courthouse, in the form of a judge that ruled in my favor with a judgment four times what I originally asked him plus attorney fees.

Yet before I could make it back home, the unimaginable happened. My former husband took his revenge against me out on our youngest daughter who had just begun her freshman year of college at Howard University in Washington, DC. The details I won't dare share unless I take her back down that dark road, but for the next two years, he deprived her of any emotional or financial support that any normal father would give and as he had faithfully done with our oldest daughter. Neither did he pay the judgment owed to me but instead appealed it all the way to the Alabama Supreme Court. He lost all three appeals but has yet to pay the judgment.

Eventually, he reached out to Sunshine in her junior year and began to help support her financially, but not before the emotional trauma and financial burden took its toll, especially during her freshman year. She worked as much as she studied during her first year at Howard and nearly lost her scholarship. The very thing I tried to protect her from, and even sacrificed my happiness for, was staring me in the face, and I couldn't change it. My Supermom cape felt void and powerless. *But God!* It wasn't done how I would or even could have done it, yet by His sufficient grace that abounded all around us, we had everything we needed (2 Corinthians 9:8). My daughter's scholarship was restored, and she mastered her sophomore year with a 4.0 average and was inducted into the Honor Society. I didn't lose my house nor have any utilities turned off, and I managed to pay off my car in full. Though I continued to accrue debt in support of my daughter's education, my credit score and I looked nothing like what I or my baby had gone through.

INSIGHT

There are times in life such as this, when we must embody the emotional, physical, and/or spiritual strength to persevere through. Yet we must realize that *when the Superwoman cape no longer fits because it becomes too large or heavy to bear, take it off, and Let God!* To "*Let God*" begins and continues with fervent prayer as offered below.

Prayer of Supplication

God, our great I AM, who is able to be any and all things we need you to be, we look to You in times like these when we feel burdened and heavy-laden by the circumstances of our lives, that we may find rest for our souls, for your Word assures us that your yoke is easy and your burden is light. Manifest your perfect strength in our lives when we grow weak and weary in our own strength and abilities, that we may feel your presence, and see the works of your hand. Help us not to be fearful of anything or anyone, but rather give us a spirit of power and sound mind, that we will have the courage and strength to walk away from whatever or whomever has us bound. In Jesus's name, we pray. Amen.

Chapter 13
Taking the Cape Off & Retaining the Strength

It hurt me to tell my twenty-eight-year-old daughter "no!" She asked me if I could go with her to Alexandria, Virginia, to help her move into her new apartment. She had just graduated from her registered nurse program, took a leap of faith in deciding to move fourteen hours from home to the DMV area, and landed an offer for her dream job, working in NICU at George Washington Hospital in DC. I was so proud of her, and everything in me wanted to go . . . but I just couldn't. It was only one week after laying my mom to rest, and *all* the emotional and physical toll it had already and would take on me was coming fast and furious. I had to return to work immediately afterward because I didn't have enough leave time to cover any more days other than the week I took to make mom's final arrangements. It would take some sho'nuff strength to pull it off! To some, it might seem that Guardian Angel was being inconsiderate or asking

too much of me, but she was just asking of me what she had seen me do many times before: be a *Superwoman*.

Still, my stomach turned as I explained that I just couldn't do it. I felt like I did when she fell and scraped her forehead just a few days before her first birthday. Her father had taken her outside with him while he was washing our car. He had placed her in the stroller, but did not buckle her in. She climbed on top of the tray and toppled over onto the cemented driveway. It was just a scrape, but it might as well have been a deep cut! As her dad came into the house rushing toward the bathroom, holding her in his arms like a football, my heart seemed to stop. I had lost Maya, miscarried a second pregnancy, and had to be on bed rest several months to keep from miscarrying Guardian Angel too. I also had held my breath throughout the night until I was assured that she would be okay, when at only two days old, her father fell asleep while holding her and she rolled off his chest to the hospital floor. So, when he rushed in with her that day, I feared that I would lose her too!

When I got to the bathroom, I saw that her little angelic forehead was "skinned all the way to the white meat" as we said when we were kids! Chills went through my entire body! I could feel the pain I imagined my baby felt. I felt her hurt then, and as I told her I couldn't go with her, I felt the hurt and disappointment I imagined she felt. And watching her eyes fill with tears as I broke the news to her didn't help at all! Yet telling her "no" was the best decision I could make for her and me at that time.

Both of my daughters have missed no opportunity to champion me as their superhero, whether in cards, social media tributes, or personalized gifts. Guardian Angel being who she is has made this explicitly clear in gifts such as the Wonder Woman embossed Mother's Day card and an oversized coffee mug labeled "Super Mama!" Even when I have made attempts at times to relinquish my Superwoman crown in their eyes, they remind me in every chance they get, that is exactly who I am to them! I remember in one card, Guardian Angel wrote, "I know you have said you are not our Superwoman, but you are to us and always will be."

Now, her Superwoman was saying "no" at one of the biggest moments in her life! As much as I yearned to be there for her as I had at every major milestone, I could no longer forsake the grace and mercy of God that had covered and protected me throughout my life, but most recently after my younger brother's death. My stress meter was past 100 when I made my way in for a routine checkup. It was just a little over a week after laying my baby brother M.T. to rest, on April 7, 2023, my fifty-fifth birthday! I chose that day not for any accolades but because it happened to be Good Friday, the best day for most of my village of friends and family to attend, and I really needed all the help I could get.

It had been a turbulent three months from his diagnosis of stage IV extensive metastatic lung cancer in the latter part of December to his death. Within a week of M.T.'s diagnosis, my mom was found nearly comatose in her home by her neighbors.

She and M.T. were hospitalized at the same time, but in different hospitals. Mom was diagnosed with diabetes and required insulin shots, which she was unable to give herself on her own. Yet she insisted on going home instead of coming to my house. She insisted on M.T. returning home with her also, and even though neither of them could effectively take care of themselves, not to mention each other, Mom didn't stop until her baby boy was back in the house with her. She was determined that she could make my brother better if he would just come back to live with her and she could cook his favorite meal: fried pork chops, white lima beans, macaroni and cheese, and cornbread, with a Sprite. But at the time of his diagnosis, his prognosis was very grim.

The months to follow were chaotic, to say the least. Two of Mom's neighbors, Jo and Nita, who were like daughters to her, happened to be caregivers and agreed to assist with her care. Mom being more concerned with M.T.'s care than her own, didn't eat as she should, which lead to frequent calls from her neighbors. It got to a point where I became anxious each time I received a call from them. Between the calls and trips back and forth to Mobile, I was doing my best to manage all my mom's business affairs and arrange for her health care needs, as well as assist with M.T.'s needs in whatever way I could, and manage my *everything*, including work a full-time job, all from Montgomery, which was two-and-a-half hours away from Mobile, where my brother and Mom lived. But this and M.T.'s death soon to follow was just a mere reflection of the "chronic stress," as one of my Sistahs termed it, that I'd been under for several years.

The turmoil I endured as M.T.'s death became imminent was just enough to tip my body's stress meter past tolerance and wellness. Within the seven days before his transition, I made three trips back and forth to Mobile. With my mother being emotionally and mentally unable to do so, I served as his next of kin and made all decisions concerning the end of his life. All of this was done while I completed a normal work week commuting an hour back and forth each day. Along with the physical toll, I endured the hurt of losing the third of four brothers in five years! This was especially tough because in the year prior to M.T.'s cancer diagnosis, his use of recreational drugs led him to behave terribly toward me, our oldest brother, and especially our mom. With the diagnosis of a terminal illness, we had been given only a short time to reconcile. I felt like I had to tuck all of it away into my *Superwoman* pocket, forgive and forget, and do what had to be done, including making his last arrangements. This would also call for preaching his eulogy that God had spoken to me just a month or so before!

None of this appeared to wear on me . . . but it had! I received a call from my doctor two days after my visit, during which she expressed concern over some of the results of my blood tests. Not only were the values of concern at critical levels, but it suggested I had cancer! **Just like with Mom, the *strength* built to keep me from breaking all these years had become the *strength* that**

was now breaking me! After researching my medical mind and my medical journals for some time, I prayed, gave it to the Lord, and committed to Him that I wouldn't take it back up again. I then went about the remainder of the weekend as normal as possible, confiding in no one except the Sistah who reminded me of the stress I'd been under and my Pastor the following Sunday after worship service, who then prayed with me. I didn't tell my daughters, my GSM, my closest friends, and especially not my mother.

My doctor recommended I come in to repeat the tests in a few days. Within twenty-four hours of repeating the blood tests, I received an email notification from Labcorp stating that my results were in. As I prepared to view the results, I closed my eyes, took a full deep breath, and I heard the Holy Spirit say, "He's about to show out again!" And show out He did! My results went from *critical* to *all normal* in seventy-two hours. The grace and mercy of God had covered me again.

It was obvious that my chronic state of stress had taken its toll. I committed to the Lord and to myself to take care of *me*. I purposely looked for ways I could reduce the stress in my life, but stress continued to find me. The next five months would become more turbulent than the months preceding my brother's death, as my mom's health began to decline rapidly. She complained repeatedly of her stomach "hurting" beginning a couple of days after Marcus's funeral. But all exams, lab tests, and x-rays at several doctor, urgent care, and emergency room visits were normal, so we chalked it up to grief. Losing three sons in five years was enough to make anyone's stomach hurt.

Yet even in her ailing, glimpses of my *Superwoman* would appear, like when the neighbors called saying she'd been working in the yard for hours! When it became clear that she could no longer live on her own, she finally agreed to move into an assisted living apartment in a senior community. It was the perfect place for her, at least I thought, next to moving to Montgomery, which she absolutely refused to do. She would get to experience some things she hadn't before, and for once in her life, someone would serve her instead of her serving others. We moved her in on August 4, 2023, and I worked as hard as I could with the help of family members and friends to make her apartment a mini version of the home she loved so well. Nevertheless, she never thrived. She continued to lose weight as she had at home, but she wasn't really eating the food either, complaining that it didn't taste good.

Each time I visited, she seemed worse rather than better, and what the staff dismissed as usual adjustment behavior changed to concerns that she was seriously ill. Meanwhile, I was making frequent trips to Mobile, taking Mom to the doctor, visiting senior communities, preparing her for the move, managing the sale of her house, and taking her to hospital visits, as the reason for her drastic decline appeared just two weeks before her death. On September 14, 2023, as I prepared for church, I received a call that she had been sent to the emergency room. As I made my way to Mobile, the hospital performed several tests, whereas the CT scan of her stomach done at the same emergency room just 2–3 months prior appeared normal, this one was not. It revealed a liver obstruction caused by a tumor on her pancreas. It was pancreatic cancer, the silent killer!

As I contemplated moving her to Montgomery for what I thought would be at least her last weeks on earth, she started bleeding on a Friday afternoon during what was supposed to be a routine medical procedure. God restored her enough for us to talk, worship, and praise Him together one last time the Saturday morning afterward, and then He called her home that same evening! For the next seven days, I would have to walk in the *strength* of a *super woman* as I had never done. As I closed her eyelids, I kissed her forehead, and whispered, "I'll see you in Glory, Momma." I immediately went into Superwoman mode.

By now I had become accustomed to making funeral arrangements for MaMa, M.J., R.L., M.T., and even helped friends with their family members' arrangements. I was so familiar with the owners of Brown Mortuary that we were on a first-name basis! As Jessica reviewed the "to-do checklist" with me, she apologized for it sounding redundant. Of course I remembered; it had only been five months since I'd chosen a casket, gathered photos, written an obituary, assembled clothing, and so on for my brother, *but this was my Momma*!

Nevertheless, I had to do it because my oldest and only remaining brother, D.W. was not going to make it to Mobile in time to help make Mom's final arrangements. I had to do it because my Mama depended on me to do it. Just a month prior to her death, she asked me about her life insurance policy and told me what to do with it when she passed away. I didn't realize it then, nor had she been diagnosed with cancer, but she knew then that it wouldn't be long. So, this was a *Superwoman* cape I had to wear because it had been tailored for me.

I did what I had to do and relied on my amazing village of friends, family, sorority sisters, and church family, who rallied around me beyond what I ever imagined. I even had to make some concessions while making the arrangements, like having to limit the repast to just family members, because we were having difficulty finding available space for the large number of people expected to attend. Although I really wanted to keep looking, thinking so many people who loved Mom and whom she loved would not get a chance to come, my pastor reminded me that I had enough on my plate. Remembering the toll stress had taken on my body after M.T.'s death, I took her advice and settled for the smaller location.

For the same reason I had to tell Guardian Angel that I couldn't go with her, "lest she be returning home to do what I had just done with my mother," I exaggerated to express the seriousness of the matter. In saying "no" to my daughter, I took off my *Superwoman* cape, yet showed myself to be a woman of *strength* just the same. In saying "no," I rebuked all the cultural myths, religious doctrines, and family traditions that "defined and confined" my ways of being a strong Black woman, wife, mother, daughter. In saying "no," I embodied the *strength* and power within to defy and deny other's expectations of me and advocate for my own well-being, in hopes that my daughter would have a different pattern of a Super woman to follow. In this pattern, I could be *strong*, even when I was in a season of weakness, "for in our weakness, His strength is made perfect. Therefore, Paul said, "I will rather boast in my infirmities, that the power of Christ may rest upon me" (2 Corinthians 12:9).

> **REFLECTION**
>
> To arrive at this point of resolution and inner strength, I had to examine the pattern of which my *Superwoman* cape was made and make the necessary alterations for a pattern that is compatible with the making of a Super Woman, two words, not one. This included my childhood upbringing, cultural practices, religious teachings, and even my own self-gratification. Oftentimes customs and traditions such as those that I was reared on are passed down through the generations without any consideration of how biased, oppressive, and nonproductive many of them are.

This is even the case with many of the Christian teachings and religious practices that I was reared on, that have either been misinterpreted or interpreted out of context, and some that simply are not Biblical nor scriptural. Of such practices and teachings, I have learned to nullify any value as a standard for being a strong godly woman, as well as Scripture interpreted or preached from a condemning, oppressive, or misogynistic context, regardless of who the messenger is.

Since my awakening in seminary, I also have committed to transforming my views concerning the role of a strong Godly woman by the constant renewal of mind through study and exegesis of Biblical text that is redeeming, liberating, and a source of strength, especially in those where women had *no choice* but to demonstrate *strength* amid adversity, disenfranchisement, and marginalization. This is the case with Queen Vashti in the Book of Esther. We often celebrate the valor Queen Esther demonstrated in risking her life to save her people, the Jews; yet if Queen Vashti hadn't mustered the courage to say "no" to having her body exploited by her drunken husband in front of his drunken friends, Esther never would have been queen.

Likewise, the Proverbs 31 woman is ritually preached as the standard for being a woman of strength and virtue, yet if examined openly and with a nonbiased lens, the Book of Joshua presents Rahab, the prostitute, as a woman of wisdom, courage, intuition, diligence, and faith just the same!

Yet, even more liberating than either of these texts, the story of Hagar in the Book of Genesis breathes life into the current situation of so many single mothers who are betrayed and deserted by their "baby's daddy," as she was by Abraham, and/or find themselves disenfranchised and ostracized by society, by no fault of their own. Yet, because of her obedience and faith in God, even in her moments of weakness, God delivered her and her son and showered their lives with favor. In these texts and many others, I find a pattern for the making of a Super Woman.

Chapter 14
Thank You, Dr. Pitters!

"THANK YOU, DR. PITTERS!" The father of my patient yelled these words at the top of his lungs as he left the pediatric practice in Montgomery, Alabama, where I was working as a nurse practitioner. I had made it clear that I was a nurse practitioner and not an MD while we were in the exam room. When he insisted, saying, "Well, you're my baby's doctor," I cautioned him about referring to me as such in public, especially in that practice because one of the male physicians had issues with nurse practitioners or other mid-level providers being referred to as "doctors." However, like with this parent, regardless of my attempts to clarify my role as an NP over the course of my career, many of my patients and/or their parents have embraced, known, and acknowledged me as their "doctor," and they have not been shy about expressing it. Still, I felt the need to clarify or justify a calling that my patients had already validated.

It just made perfect sense. It was the terminal degree of my profession, and at least when they call me "doctor," it will be legitimately correct, I rationalized. So, I began contemplating my return to school to pursue a Doctor of Nursing, especially when the Alabama Board of Nursing proposed making it the

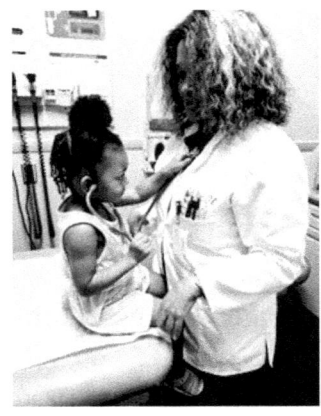

degree requirement for incoming nurse practitioners. Several of my colleagues had already begun working toward that goal, which added additional pressure for me to do the same, or at least I felt so. Although it would not be required of me to continue to practice as an NP nor have any influence whatsoever on my scope of practice or salary, that "Alpha" trait within that pushes me to excel in whatever I do, wouldn't let me rest unless I pursued that degree.

Others even encouraged me to go further to medical school to obtain my MD, reasoning that I was so close or that with my personality, I'd be the best "doctor." My GSM even committed to help care for my youngest daughter while I was in school. Yet, unlike what I'd done with obtaining my master's degree, I procrastinated with applying and starting that process. I remember hearing my pastor say, when I deliberated between a two-year or three-year Doctor of Nursing track, "It's not about the three years; the three years will come and go regardless." Though I was convinced that earning a doctorate in some manner as a medical professional was the path in my pursuit of excellence to take, in July 2016, I committed to the Lord that if He provided a way, I would go to seminary. He did, and I enrolled as a student at the Interdenominational Theological Center (ITC) in Atlanta, Georgia, in January 2017.

What da? That's the question I'm sure many within my smaller and greater circle had, and with the question came doubt, and with doubt disapproval, and for some even disappointment. My village supported me as a village does, especially my GSM who faithfully helped care for my child. I am forever grateful for her and so many others. Yet I just felt like there were no pompoms or pep rallies, like I thought would have been present if I had pursued a doctorate in medicine or nursing. They would have been able to say my friend, sister, niece . . . is a "doctor." It was I who would have to do the work for either. Still, I felt that to many, I had failed to meet the "superwoman" expectations they had for me. But there was another "cape" prepared for me to wear. It, too, carried a heavy weight. For three-and-a-half years, I functioned as a full-time student and full-time nurse practitioner, working five days a week! Two months after beginning seminary, my second-oldest brother R.L. passed away suddenly from a massive stroke and brain hemorrhage. It had only been seven months since M.T. had passed away from a heart attack. What was God doing?

Most of my classes were online, but to meet the required thirty hours of on-campus courses, I started traveling back and forth to class after the first semester. Initially, I took advantage of the one-week fast track and weekend courses, but to finish in four years or less, as I hoped to do, I also had to start taking evening classes held on weekdays. I usually worked a half day, then made a same day round trip to Atlanta, returning home usually around

10:30 p.m. All of this in the midst of the nasty child support court battle with my ex-husband. During one of my one-week fast track courses, I had to leave very early in the morning, drive from Atlanta to Huntsville, Alabama, for depositions and go back to Atlanta for my evening class. My ex-husband insisted on the depositions as a ploy to delay the proceedings and escalate my lawyer fees. However, the judge ordered the depositions to be held in her courtroom because he had purposely been noncompliant in adherence to court deadlines and dates. Oh! And then there was the COVID-19 pandemic!

Yet in all the tribulation, there was purpose. Seminary was exactly where I needed to be at that time and at ITC! It was never about the degree, nor so much about the academics but the spiritual journey with God while I was going through the process of earning the degree. Having started the journey feeling spiritually broken and lost concerning my walk as a minister, I found wholeness and divine guidance during the time I was there. I could hear God clearer and gained a clear vision of my mission as a minister and messenger of God.

While I was not affirmed as a minister by my home church, my fellow seminarians welcomed me into fellowship and affirmed God's call on my life without question or witness from day one. Little did they know, they were the angels God charged with keeping my limp wings lifted until I gained the strength to fly again. I graduated magna cum laude with a Master of Divinity three-and-a-half years later, in May 2020, just in time to devote all of my attention and time toward my baby daughter's senior year of high school.

I never really discerned what my pastor meant by "it's not about the three years," because I didn't ask. But this is what I heard from the Lord when again, some three years later, I began to deliberate between obtaining a Doctor of Nursing or a Doctor of Ministry degree. During an intense period of two weeks, in work, church, and lay settings, the words, "Dr. Pitters" seemed to be reverberating in my ears! Not just by my patients and/or their parents, but now even professionals who understood quite well what degrees I had and my role as an NP, publicly addressed me as such! When I explained to the interpreter at work that she didn't have to refer to me as "Dr. Pitters," because I was an NP, the next morning she greeted me the same. I heard the Lord say, "How much more time, money, and heart are you going to spend justifying a calling that I not only have validated but also glorified in the eyes of the people?"

A few days later, during our church's Sisterhood Ministry event, Rev. Dr. Kathy McFadden (2023) presented from her book *Unstuck*. She shared that our choices should not be bound by what other people think we should do. That evening, I committed to God that if He provided a way, I would pursue a Doctorate in Ministry. Because the truth of the whole matter is, I delayed and deterred getting the Doctor of Nursing because I had no desire to do the work it took to earn it. I love what I do as a health care provider and am very good at it, but over the years, I realized that the position had just become the platform for me to do a greater work as a messenger of God, which had become my heart's desire.

I once told my pastor in previous years that "ministry was everything to me," meaning I see God in everything! I enjoy using creativity to reveal God to others. During the last year of seminary, I chose nontraditional ministry settings to complete my senior Capstone ministry project and my chaplain intern hours. Over the years, I have found myself offering hope and spiritual guidance to my patients and coworkers. What dwells in me now is a growing desire to do more of it.

I came to realize, as my beloved professor Dr. Itihari Toure enlightened me during seminary, that though the two professions of nurse practitioner and minister were separate, the calling was one in the same. I even began to petition God to reconcile the two professions into one practice setting, as I looked toward transitioning to a less stressful work setting. To anyone else (and sometimes even to me) it makes absolutely no sense to even consider the Doctor of Ministry. But I found, as the Psalmist declares, when you "delight yourself in the Lord, He will give you the desires of your heart." Once I committed to the Lord that I would pursue a Doctorate in Ministry in November 2023, He began to open pathways to seminaries with Doctor of Ministry in Spiritual Direction programs.

> **INSIGHT**
>
> In the making of a Super Woman, there are times you must take off or relinquish the superwoman roles others impose on you so you can walk in that which God has ordained for you to wear. *Listen to your heart.* If it is God's will for your life, He will give you a desire or yearning for it. When the prophet Jeremiah declared he would not declare the word of the Lord to the people anymore, because they rejected him, the Bible says that "then in his *heart* it became as a burning fire shut up in his bones" (Jeremiah 20:9). If still in doubt, through prayer ask God to give you clarity and guidance. I commit to you as with me, He will.

Chapter 15
A Super Woman Pattern: Maintaining Purpose, Peace, and Balance

At the end of one of my recent counseling sessions, shortly before finishing this book, my counselor assessed my progress in managing my grief and anxiety as she periodically had done since I started. She noted in her assessment that I was doing well in "maintaining purpose, peace, and balance." If I had to create a pattern or template for the making of a Super Woman (or person) based on insights I've gained from these and other life experiences, that would be it. To effectively use one's gifts, talents, and strengths to navigate through life's crises and remain emotionally and spiritually whole, one must be able to maintain purpose, peace, and balance.

Having lived life as I have, I'm careful to always be mindful of the *grace* of God that has covered me throughout my life. In the midst of tribulations, it is what gives me *peace* of mind and spirit regardless of how challenging the circumstances of my current reality might be. Being able to reflect on the goodness of God gives me contentment that if God has covered me with his abundant grace countless times before, surely God will do it again.

I am reminded of the rhetorical question asked by Paul in Romans 8:31, which reads, "What must we say to these things? If God be for us, who can be against us?" Looking back at these and other life experiences, I can testify to Paul's bold arrogance. Reason being, while the testing of my character in many of these events yielded strength and resilience that has gotten me through some very difficult times in my life, especially within the past few years, I realize that there was always an element of God's *grace* present! Even before I understood what *grace* was or could appreciate it and even when the *Superwoman* in me jeopardized my health and well-being, the grace of God has always been knocking on my door.

This was the case as the due date for the last payment of my lawyer's retainer was rapidly approaching. I had just said to my GSM that I was waiting on something *big*. However, just a day or two later, I spent most of the afternoon working on my application to renew my mortgage loan and became somber by the amount of debt I had accrued during the recent years of legal battle with my ex-husband. Nevertheless, I devised a plan to get it all done, and though it unfortunately would increase my debt even more, I was resolved to persevere through it.

While in the shower shortly thereafter, I heard my doorbell ring. When I got out of the shower and checked my doorbell camera's video, I saw that a dear friend had stopped by and placed something under my flowerpot. When I called her, she was still in her car outside of my house. She said she stopped by because she had received a financial blessing and wanted to bless me as well. I was in awe of God's perfect timing! Overcome with humility and gratitude at the wonderfulness and faithfulness of God, I shared with my friend the reason I was so grateful. She then made a trip to her car and blessed me even more when she returned! So many times, God has made a way for me such as this that I cannot recall them all.

Therefore, in my journey to walk in the will of God for my life, I have learned how to embrace such *grace* unapologetically! As the songwriter Dr. Bill Winston wrote, "favor ain't fair, but it sure feels fabulous!" Yet I am careful to give God all the glory and honor due Him unless I become too arrogant and confident in my own abilities. I'm never ashamed to tell others that the reason I don't look like any of the emotional or physical trauma I have been through is by the *grace* of God! Unearned. Unmerited. Favor.

Being always mindful of God's grace, I also strive to walk worthily and purposefully in the natural and spiritual gifts he has anointed me with. The Bible teaches us that each of us are given spiritual gifts, that we may be of help to others (I Cor. 12:7). The Message Bible reads the same verse as, "Each person is given something to do that shows who God is." For the rest of my life, I'm committed to doing just that. Having experienced the unmerited favor of God on my life, I cannot afford to waste another day, hour, or minute without intent and effort to do what

God created and anointed me to do. *PeriodT*! To do otherwise is to forsake my divine purpose for being here.

I am uncle Sunny's "little smart girl" and Uncle Bubba's "phenomenal woman!" I am a Super Woman; two words, not one! In the words of one of my spiritual brothers, "I am badass!" LOL! Nevertheless, I have not always embraced the intellectual and spiritual gifts God has anointed me with. For example, during the initial unrest of my marriage, I questioned whether my use of such gifts and strengths lead my former husband to turn to another woman. During the first few years of our marriage, I had shown the ability to be both the breadwinner and homemaker—bring home the bacon and cook it too, make the beds in the house, and maintain the flowerbeds outside as well, mop the kitchen floor, and lay tile on the porch foyer, and much more. Had this show of strength lead him to stray, I wondered?

I learned thereafter that infidelity is not about the other person's inadequacies, but more about the unfaithful person's own feeling of inadequacy and insecurity. This became clear during an early marriage counseling session before his infidelity was confirmed by the birth of his son, when the counselor asked us to identify those attributes that initially attracted us to each other. A few sessions later, he asked us what it was about each other that we now were displeased with. After we both shared our undesirables concerning each other, the counselor referred to his notes from the initial session, then said to my ex-husband,

"That's strange . . . these are the same attributes you initially found attractive in Coretta!"

During the remaining years of the marriage, and especially after the divorce, I gradually grew to embrace my God-given talents and spiritual gifts, regardless of what insecurities he or anyone else might have. However, I would have to learn in the years to come how to gauge my use of those gifts to protect my sanity and my physical well-being. As I prepared to close my mom's casket at her homegoing celebration, I said to my two daughters who were holding on to my arms in support, "Turn me loose, I'm good." At that moment, there were no feelings of sorrow. I had cried and would cry later, sometimes even now, but at that moment, I felt no need to cry, so I didn't. God had strengthened me along the journey to do all that I could, and in that moment gave me the emotional, spiritual, and physical fortitude to celebrate her life with joy, happiness, and peace.

I obviously had been prepared for that moment; nonetheless, the totality of it all would eventually take its toll on my health and well-being as it had after M.T.'s death, unless I did something to restore balance in my life. My mind and body had been in *Superwoman* gear that entire year, so much so that when I finally had time to sleep, I found it difficult to do so. I began grief counseling shortly thereafter to effectively process the loss of my mother and three brothers. Since then, I have also found it to be a conducive environment for processing the loss of my father, my failed marriage, and so much more. Seeking professional counseling has been one of the best decisions I've made in life. It has been a practical and effective tool for helping me balance a life of purpose and peace.

I look forward to my "get *the-ra-pied* sessions!" It has become an act of self-care, a time set aside for *me*. Yet to "maintain purpose, peace, and balance" during this turbulent time in my life, I also had to measure the value of carrying out every task asked or desired of me. Even though I had *no choice* but to return to work only two days after Mom's funeral, because I didn't have any more paid leave to use, I could, however, gauge my time spent in other areas. This included social activities, such as those hosted by my beloved AKA sorority. I attended some, but others had to pass me by. I even declined some ministry invitations.

To restore balance between walking in purpose and maintaining my peace, I also had to say no to others and to myself. Standards I once held in high regard, I no longer prioritized as I had before. Household chores, indoors and outdoors had to wait, and while my mom was surely turning in her grave, I learned to just turn my head away from whatever was left undone, whether it was mountains of dust buildup, stacks of unpacked boxes, or untrimmed shrubbery. Months later, when my finances could afford it, I hired someone to help me clean, which likely caused another gravitational shift in Mom's resting place! LOL! When I considered doing this when she was living, she would say, "Why hire someone when you got me?" Moving forward I've committed to budgeting funds monthly for housekeeping help as another act of self-care, and I feel no less of a Super Woman for doing so.

Lastly, to walk worthily in my God-ordained purpose, I am now determined to *embrace* the *journey* within! Early in the morning of June 22, 2024, I was abruptly awakened around 2:30 a.m., and I heard the Spirit of the Lord say, "I'm about to elevate you." Hearing it clearly, I laid back down and went to sleep. My response was not to be dismissive of what I heard, because I know the faithfulness of God; I just didn't expect it to happen the same day! Yet that's exactly what happened!

Later as I arose for the workday, an email alert sent just four hours after that early morning encounter with God caught my attention as I prepared to read my daily devotion. The heading of the email read, "Congratulations, Coretta, on your nomination!!!" It went on to say, "We are honored to inform you that The Herprenuer Network International has selected you to receive The Medical Award at The HER Awards Alabama 2024." Amazed by the spontaneity of it all, I screamed, "God, you have got to be kidding!" As I read on, I realized that the founder and president of the organization was a woman I had just encountered for the first time at work a couple of weeks before and was stunned even more.

I began to ponder just how this could have happened. Surely, she could not have been that impressed with my work performance, my analytical mind calculated, as if I were not worthy of such honor. The HER award honors and celebrates the work of Christian women in ministry, service, and business, as

I had been faithfully doing for years. Not that I was seeking or even expecting such honor for my work and service, but as a male friend and colleague expressed, I deserved to be among the elite list of women being honored. Yet I questioned how this could be because it didn't fit into my reasonable thought process or occur according to my timeline.

In my deliberation, I did not respond to the invitation by the requested deadline. However, a couple of weeks later, *grace* and *mercy* came knocking on my door again when the president of the organization reached out to me and extended the invitation to me again. Lesson learned! As I prepare to accept this honor within days of submitting this memoir for publication, and all that God has planned for me, I close with this insight for *embracing* the *journey*.

INSIGHT

In my negligence to readily accept the HER award, I heard the Lord say, "What business of yours is it when, where, how, or who I use to elevate you?" I understood then that with God, I didn't have to *fight like a girl* anymore! I don't have to outthink him or try to compensate for weaknesses I think I may have, nor prove anything to anyone, including me, only just accept and trust in his sovereign will and divine providence concerning my life. Making it plain, this meant I must:

1. Demonstrate a willingness to conform to his plan by the renewal of preset ideas, traditions, and thought processes, instead of trying to conform his plan to mine. It would never fit anyway, for "God's thoughts are not our thoughts nor are his ways our ways," the Bible tells us (Isaiah 55:8).
2. Dismiss or silence doubts and negative thoughts during seasons of trial and tribulation, realizing that during the journey to becoming a Super Woman there will be such times, yet being confident that seasons do change. For as Ecclesiastes Chapter 2 teaches, with the season of tribulation, a season of triumph is to follow.
3. Always be ready to run within God's omnipresent timing, for God's vision for our lives "is yet for an appointed time . . . [and] even though it delays . . . it will certainly come; [then] it will not delay" (Habakkuk 2:3 AMP).